Stratford Library Association
2203 Main Street
Stratford, CT 06615
203-385-4160

*United States Presidents*

# John Quincy Adams

**Series Consultant:**
*Don M. Coerver, professor of history*
*Texas Christian University, Fort Worth, Texas*

Jane C. Walker

**Enslow Publishers, Inc.**

40 Industrial Road         PO Box 38
Box 398             Aldershot
Berkeley Heights, NJ 07922  Hants GU12 6BP
USA                      UK
http://www.enslow.com

## Acknowledgments

*Adams National Historic Park: Kelly Peterson Cobble; Episcopal Church of the Redeemer: Reverend Cindy Baskin; First Parish Church of Quincy: Reverend Shelden Benton; Massachusetts Historical Society: Chris Steele.*

**Library of Congress Cataloging-in-Publication Data**

Walker, Jane C.
    John Quincy Adams / Jane C. Walker.
      p. cm. — (United States presidents)
    Includes bibliographical references and index.
    Summary: Examines the life of the sixth president of the United States, including his childhood, marriage, and career as a debater, writer, and politician.
    ISBN 0-7660-1161-5
    1. Adams, John Quincy, 1767–1848—Juvenile literature.
    2. Presidents—United States—Biography—Juvenile literature.
    [1. Adams, John Quincy, 1767–1848. 2. Presidents.] I. Title.
    II. Series.
    E377.W16   2000
    973.5'5'092–dc21
    [B]                        98-46379
                                 CIP
                                 AC

Printed in the United States of America

10 9 8 7 6 5 4 3 2 1

**To Our Readers:**
All Internet addresses in this book were active and appropriate when we went to press. Any comments or suggestions can be sent by e-mail to Comments@enslow.com or to the address on the back cover.

**Illustration Credits:** Adams National Historical Park, pp. 29, 43, 45, 58, 95, 97, 100; © Corel Corporation, p. 60; Jane C. Walker, pp. 12 (bottom), 114, 118; Library of Congress, pp. 4, 12 (top), 19, 35, 62, 76, 82, 85, 105, 113; Massachusetts Historical Society, p. 15; Reproduced from *The American Revolution, A Picture Sourcebook*, Dover Publications, Inc., 1975, pp. 6, 7, 16; Robert M. Friedman, p. 109.

**Source Document Credits:** Adams Historical Park, p. 69; Massachusetts Historical Society, p. 27, 102; Library of Congress, p. 48.

**Cover Illustration:** Library of Congress.

# Contents

*This lithograph depicts John Quincy Adams at about the time of the beginning of his presidency in 1825.*

# 1

# BUNKER HILL

**A**t three o'clock in the morning on Saturday, June 17, 1775, young John Quincy Adams snapped awake when he heard the roar of cannon fire. His mother, Abigail, heard it, too. By now, seven-year-old Johnny, as the boy was called, was used to the noisy roar. Cannon fire had been thundering nearby for two months. The American colonists were at war against their mother country, Great Britain. They were fighting for their political and human rights.

Later that same day, Abigail took her son outside to see what was happening. Mother and son crossed the dirt road in front of their home in Braintree, Massachusetts, and climbed Penn's Hill, which lay across the road. From atop a granite slate slab on Penn's Hill they could see all the way across Boston Bay to Charlestown, Massachusetts,

*This panoramic view of the Battle of Bunker Hill was published shortly after the historic battle took place.*

where a huge cloud of black smoke was now blocking out what used to be the homes and church spires of a peaceful city. The British had burned Charlestown to the ground.

The Battle of Bunker Hill, as the Charlestown battle soon was referred to, actually took place on Breed's Hill. Both hills were part of Charlestown, and often they were mistaken for each other. During this historic battle in the American Revolution, the Americans forced the British to retreat twice. After the second retreat, however, the Americans ran out of ammunition. The British charged a third time, and this time they defeated the Americans. However, their victory was costly: Great Britain's dead and wounded numbered 1,054 soldiers. American casualties totaled 441, and of those only 100 had been killed.[1]

One of the Americans killed in the battle was Dr. Joseph Warren, the Adams's friend and physician. Only the day before, Dr. Warren had set Johnny's fractured forefinger. The loss of such a dear friend brought the brutality of the war even closer to home.

With his father, John Adams, away much of the time working for the American colonists' rebel cause against the British, young Johnny had assumed the responsibilities of the man of the house. He helped his mother with the other children, the daily household chores, and even her political activities. Like her husband, Abigail Adams was a devoted patriot.

In June of 1775, John Adams was in Philadelphia, Pennsylvania, serving as Massachusetts' delegate to the

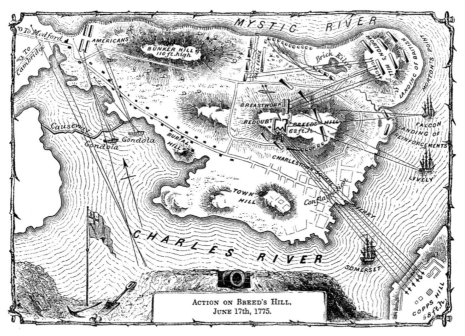

*The military action that took place on Breed's Hill on June 17, 1775, is shown on this map.*

Continental Congress. The Congress was trying to negotiate the American colonists' disputes with Great Britain. Abigail wrote letters to her husband reporting the latest war information, which she had observed from the hill and learned through the town's gossip. She was John's eyes and ears, his "intelligence," his spy. In addition, because the Adams's farmhouse backed onto a road leading to Boston, riders often stopped there to deliver important news about battles and political activities. Sometimes the riders spent the night, sheltered by Abigail's warm hospitality.

Johnny, too, was a spy. His mother had her son ride into Boston regularly to deliver and receive mail. While in Boston, Johnny would observe and count the number of British soldiers. Then he would report his findings back to his mother. In turn, Abigail would write to her husband about what Johnny had noted on his mail routes.[2]

Throughout the year of 1775, Johnny watched his mother live in fear. The Adams's home was not far from British-controlled Boston. The constant threat of British soldiers invading and possibly destroying their home was frighteningly real.

John Quincy never forgot the day he stood with his mother on the hill, witnessing the important Battle of Bunker Hill. It was a turning point in the American Revolution, and marked a conscious dedication in the boy to the cause of freedom and the principles for which the war was being fought.

# 2

# TO BE A PATRIOT

The Adamses had lived in the Massachusetts Bay colony since 1636, when Henry Adams received a land grant in Braintree from Great Britain's king, Charles I. The Adams line gained social clout when Joseph II Adams married Hannah Bass. Her grandparents, John and Priscilla Alden, were two of the first English pilgrims to arrive in the new land. Legend states that John Alden was actually the first person to step off the ship *Mayflower* onto Plymouth Rock.

Joseph II and Hannah's second son, John, was a farmer during the growing and harvesting seasons and a shoemaker in the winter. He married Susanna Boylston, a granddaughter of a prominent English physician and a niece of Zabdiel Boylston, a physician who introduced the smallpox vaccine into North America. John and Susanna lived in and owned two adjacent homes with their farmland in Braintree (renamed Quincy in 1792).

John and Susanna Adams had three sons. As was the custom of the day, the eldest son was to attend college and forego his father's trade for a profession in law, medicine, or divinity. John, Sr., spent many years saving his money so John, Jr., could get a college education. However, John, Jr., had a strong love for farming, and he pleaded with his father to let him do the hard labor of the land rather than attend college. Despite his pleas, John, Jr., was sent to Harvard College and graduated in 1755.

Afterward, he chose law to be his profession, since he had discovered a passion for public speaking at Harvard. John, Jr.'s father had not managed to save enough money for him to apprentice with, or study under, a lawyer. Therefore, to pay his way through his law apprenticeship, John, Jr., earned money by teaching boys at the one-room schoolhouse in Worcester.

After completing his two-year apprenticeship, John Adams, Jr., officially became a Massachusetts lawyer on November 6, 1758. Three years later his father died, leaving John one of the two houses and one third of the farmland he owned in Braintree.

Despite this inheritance and his love for farming, John stuck with the law. His legal cases were scattered across the Massachusetts Bay colony, so John traveled from town to town, working with his clients. His circuit law practice, as it was called, eventually brought him to Weymouth's Congregational church, where he first met fifteen-year-old Abigail Smith, the second daughter of the Reverend William Smith. At that time, John was not much interested in Abigail, who was ten years his junior, but a few years later business once again took him to the same church. This time, John's feelings for Abigail had changed, and the couple began a serious courtship.[1] Abigail was spirited, intelligent, and highly opinionated, and John admired these qualities, which were unusual for a woman of the times. On Thursday, October 25, 1764, twenty-nine-year-old John Adams married nineteen-year-old Abigail Smith at her home, the church parsonage.

John and Abigail lived in the saltbox-shaped home that John had inherited from his father. Saltbox-shaped homes were popular in New England because the roofs were designed to slope sharply downward from the south side to the north side of each house, causing snow to fall off the top. The first floor consisted of a parlor, an office for John's work, a small room for the housemaid, and a large kitchen built around a fireplace. A wooden staircase led to the second floor, which provided two large bedrooms and two low-ceilinged children's bedrooms. So modest was the house that Abigail often wished she had a small room with a window for her own privacy.[2] Next door was the house where John had been born. His mother still lived there with his stepfather.

John spent most of his time away from home pursuing his court cases. While her husband was gone, Abigail managed the farm and wrote letters to him. Because Abigail lacked a formal education, her letters contained many examples of incorrect grammar and spelling. Nevertheless, she kept John informed about the farm's progress and asked him agricultural questions.

In 1765, Great Britain placed a Stamp Act on the American colonists. The act taxed all newspapers, legal documents, and other papers that were printed in the British-owned American colonies. Many American

*A nineteenth-century drawing shows John Quincy Adams's birthplace (left). The house next door (below) was the birthplace of John Quincy's father, John Adams. These are the oldest American presidential birthplaces.*

colonists like John and Abigail Adams resented Great Britain's tax. They believed that the colonies should be represented in the British Parliament, or government, if they were to pay taxes. Colonists who fought against British rule were called patriots. Some of the more radical patriots formed a group called the Sons of Liberty. John Adams was a charter member of this group. Abigail supported and agreed with her husband's political views.

That same year a daughter named Abigail, nicknamed Nabby, was born to the Adamses. Two years later, their first son was born on July 11, 1767. Abigail named him John Quincy after Colonel John Quincy, her grandfather. His parents called him Johnny during his childhood.

At the time of Johnny's birth, the American colonists had forced the repeal of the hated Stamp Act of 1765 that had been imposed on them by the British Parliament. However, in 1767, the British government replaced the canceled Stamp Act with the Townshend Acts. These acts required the payment of import taxes by the colonists on glass, paint, tea, and wine.

When Johnny was a year old, his father suggested the family move to Boston, where he could be close to his family, his law clients, and the growing political activity swirling about the colonies. This would be the first of a series of moves between Braintree and Boston.

Therefore, in 1768, John and Abigail Adams rented a white house on Brattle Square in Boston. Abigail gave birth to a second daughter, named Susanna, who was nicknamed Suky. Unlike rural Braintree, the city bustled with activity. Each morning, the red-uniformed British soldiers pounded their drums and tooted their fifes during the daily drills. Horse-drawn carriages clattered over the cobblestones, vendors displayed their goods, and crowds gathered in the streets. At night a watchman called out each hour.

In February of 1770, Suky died. Since birth Suky had been a sickly baby and her survival had always seemed unpredictable. Neither of the child's parents could bear to write in their diaries about their daughter's death.

A month after Suky's death, a snowfall covered the city of Boston. On the evening of March 5, 1770, John Adams walked across the fresh fallen snow to attend a political meeting. As he walked, he noticed boys, young men, and British soldiers milling in the streets. Shortly after 9:00 P.M., he heard the crack of gunfire and the clanging of bells. Thinking that the bells were signaling a fire, John and the other men ran outside the meeting hall to help. Instead, they learned that the bells were a call for the colonists to take up arms. The red-uniformed British, sometimes mockingly called "lobsters" or "bloody backs," had shot and killed five Bostonians. The Bostonians had provoked these British soldiers by throwing snowballs and oyster shells at them.

Safe in their white house, Abigail and her two children also heard the gunfire. They rushed to the window and saw British soldiers running down the street. Three-year-old Johnny begged to go outside and see what was happening, but Abigail marched both of the children back to bed. Soon John ran home to see if his family was safe.

The next day the British soldiers were charged with the murders of the five Bostonians. Angry colonists demanded that the British soldiers be hanged for their crime. Boston lawyers were reluctant to defend the murderers in such an emotional case. Yet under the law, even British subjects were entitled to a fair trial. Although he was risking his reputation as a lawyer, John Adams stood up to his fellow Bostonians and agreed to represent the British soldiers in this case, which soon became known as the Boston Massacre. He strongly believed that all men had the right to defend themselves.

In court, John Adams brought forth evidence to show that the colonial boys and men had indeed threatened the British soldiers and that their retaliation had been

*The Boston Massacre occurred on March 5, 1770, when British soldiers (on the right) fired on a crowd of Boston citizens (left). This illustration was engraved by Paul Revere shortly after the event.*

provoked. John proved that the British soldiers were simply protecting themselves, and he won the case.

Later that same year, Abigail gave birth to a second son, Charles; and two years later, in 1772, a third son, Thomas Boylston, was born. During those two years, tempers in Boston and in the other colonies continued to flare. In 1773 the British government, in an effort to remedy the East India Company's overstocked warehouses of tea, allowed the company to sell tea directly to the colonists. This action deprived the American merchants, who normally bought the tea from the British and sold it to the colonists, from making a profit. To make matters worse, a tax on importing tea was also imposed. Finally the colonial merchants retaliated. On December 16, 1773, John's cousin Samuel Adams and other merchants, disguised as Mohawk Indians, crept aboard British ships docked in the harbor and dumped chests of tea overboard in protest.

People began to call this incident the Boston Tea Party. The British Parliament ordered the people of Boston to pay for the tea, but the colonists refused. In response, the British closed the port of Boston to all trade and travel in an attempt to punish the American colonies for failing to follow their orders. However, the British only succeeded in escalating the colonists' anger against them.

In 1774, representatives from each of the thirteen colonies met in Philadelphia to talk about whether the British Parliament had the right to pass laws on behalf of

*On December 16, 1773, a band of Bostonians, disguised rather crudely as American Indians, boarded three British ships carrying tea. They threw overboard 342 chests of tea in protest against the British attempt to tax tea imported to America.*

the colonies or whether they could legally force the colonies to pay taxes. John Adams was elected to be one of the five representatives from Massachusetts to attend the First Continental Congress in Philadelphia.

John Adams had been gone only a year when he decided to move his family back to Braintree. He was worried about the increasing presence of British troops in Boston. On April 19, 1775, British soldiers and American patriots exchanged musket shots on the green in Lexington, Massachusetts. The American Revolutionary War had officially begun.

John remained absent from his home most of the time; he was consumed with work both for the Continental Congress and his circuit law practice. However, despite his prolonged absences, John remained a constant influence on his children. He believed strongly in the power and importance of education, and he personally outlined the school curriculum for his children. In a letter to Abigail, he wrote, " . . . The minds and manners of our Children. . . . Let us teach them not only to do virtuously but to excel. To excel they must be steady, active, and industrious."[3] The curriculum that John suggested for his children included classes in French, history, philosophy, Latin, and Greek. However, for enjoyable reading matter, Johnny chose his own literature: fairy tales and adventure stories like *The Arabian Nights*. When his mother was not looking, Johnny sometimes borrowed his father's tobacco pipe and, imitating his father, smoked while he read.[4]

When Braintree's public schools were disrupted by the revolutionary war, Johnny's mother became his teacher. Abigail added morality lessons to her children's schooling. She saw that Johnny was a bright, spirited child, much like herself, who needed the proper direction to distinguish good from evil. To teach her son morality, Abigail had Johnny read and memorize stories about Little Giles Gingerbread, an honest, poor boy, who learned to read and was taught moral values. These values consisted of duty to family and society, religion, virtue, hard work, and the love of learning. Johnny loved these stories and learned many of his values from them.

While Nabby and Johnny studied safely in Braintree, many Bostonians were fleeing their city. Many of these refugees were given temporary shelter by Abigail and her neighbors. Like her husband, Abigail Adams strongly supported the American Revolution. American soldiers, called "minutemen" because they would fight with only a minute's notice, often knocked at her door asking for food and lodging. Abigail helped the soldiers, risking her life by doing so: Had the British caught her harboring their enemies, they would have hanged her. Johnny supported his mother's patriotic position. In the mornings, the boy marched alongside the minutemen during their drill.

Each night Abigail led Johnny in a two-part prayer. First they recited together the Lord's Prayer, then the poem "Ode" by William Collins, which glorified soldiers who had died fighting a 1745 rebellion in Great Britain. Abigail firmly believed that defending one's rights and property was an appeal to God. Like many patriots, she believed the war to be an act of Divine Providence. Providence is the belief that God guides history through the actions of people in order to fulfill His plan for creation. A person's duty is to be obedient to God. Through her example, Abigail taught Johnny faith in Divine Providence, or God's plans.

Wartime meant death, but not all deaths were caused

by fighting. Diseases like dysentery and smallpox spread quickly during the revolution. The constant movement and poor sanitation of soldiers and civilians contributed to the spread of the diseases. John Adams wrote to his wife: "The Small Pox is ten times more terrible than Britons, Canadians, and Indians together."[5]

When the British were finally expelled from Boston in 1776, Abigail decided to take her family there to be inoculated, or vaccinated, against smallpox. She and her four children moved into Uncle Isaac Smith's Boston mansion. The home would serve as an isolation hospital, since people who were inoculated temporarily became carriers of the disease. Smallpox inoculation was a simple yet dangerous procedure. The physician would slit a small incision into the arm, insert a mild strain of smallpox pus, bandage the incision, and then have the patient wait for the smallpox symptoms to

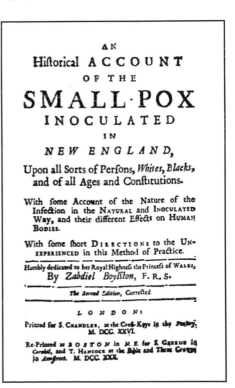

*Zabdiel Boylston and Cotton Mather experimented with a smallpox vaccine. Because people feared it would give them the disease, it was very unpopular, although effective. This history is the last of several books written by the two physicians on the subject. It represents the first written presentation of a clinical experiment by an American physician.*

appear. Hopefully, the inoculated individual would receive a mild case of the disease, and thus become immune from ever contracting smallpox again.

While waiting at Uncle Isaac's mansion for the smallpox symptoms to materialize, Abigail proudly listened to the Declaration of Independence being read for the first time from the State House balcony. Her husband was one of five men who had drawn up this important document. Although Thomas Jefferson had written most of it, John had contributed many of the ideas. After the reading, Abigail watched Boston patriots strip Great Britain's royal symbols from the State House.

A few days later, the smallpox symptoms appeared. Abigail, Johnny, and Thomas Boylston had mild reactions, but Nabby and Charles suffered heavily. Nabby's face was permanently scarred from the pox, and Charles was delirious with fever for two days. When everyone had finally recovered, the family returned home to Braintree.

As the war continued, families prepared for the worst. On one occasion, Johnny walked into his house and spotted his mother dropping her pewter spoons into a large kettle. Johnny's uncle, Elihu Adams, dressed in a minuteman's uniform, stood waiting while Abigail worked, his musket slung across his back. Johnny finally realized that his mother was melting the spoons to make bullets, and he experienced a sudden burst of patriotic pride. Sixty-eight years later, John Quincy Adams would recall the incident in a letter to a friend, saying "Do you wonder that a boy of seven who witnessed this scene should be a patriot?"[6]

# 3

# LESSONS ABROAD

On October 17, 1777, British general John Burgoyne surrendered after several unsuccessful attempts to break through American lines at Saratoga, New York. This victory was a turning point for the American colonists, because it drew allied France into sending troops and fleets of ships to their side.

On November 28, 1777, John Adams received a letter from Congress asking him to be one of three American commissioners to France. Their purpose would be to draft a treaty of military alliance and mutual commerce. Although John hated to leave his family so soon after his stay in Philadelphia, he accepted the position. John believed that duty to one's country came first. As usual, Abigail firmly shared her husband's belief and supported his decision to go to France.

Ten-year-old Johnny begged to accompany his father.

John had thought seriously about taking his family with him to France, but he feared they might be hurt in the crossfire of maritime warfare. Besides, Congress had not allotted enough money to cover all of their expenses. However, Johnny continued to plead with his father. He could learn French firsthand and help with his father's clerical work. Abigail was torn. She understood that the boy needed to be with his father. Johnny hardly knew his father because so much of his work took him away from home. Finally, Abigail gave her blessing for her son to go. She reminded him "never to disgrace his mother, and to behave worthily of his father."[1]

Father and son boarded the frigate *Boston* on February 13, 1778. Five days into their ocean voyage they spotted three British ships. The *Boston* captain, Samuel Tucker, feared that British intelligence had found out about John Adams's mission, and that the British ships intended to capture the *Boston*. Knowing that his ship was undermanned and the crew poorly trained, Captain Tucker chose to run instead of fight. A naval disaster was thus avoided. Two days and one night later, the winds died and the skies darkened. The *Boston*'s crew now encountered a new and more fearsome enemy—a gulf stream storm. For three days gale winds thrashed the frigate, killing three sailors. John was surprised and proud that his ten-year-old son showed no sign of strain or fear.[2] Finally, after six weeks of hazardous travel, the *Boston* arrived in France.

John Adams met the other two American commissioners, Benjamin Franklin and Arthur Lee, in Paris. Franklin and Lee had already completed most of the treaty on alliance and commerce, but John found that the commissioners were spending far too much money and had kept no account books. While his father straightened out the bookkeeping, Johnny started school at *Le Coeur,* a boarding school in nearby Passy, France.

The school day began at six in the morning. Johnny's classes consisted of dancing, fencing, music, drawing, Latin, and French. He ate all of his meals at the boarding school and went to bed every night at eight o'clock. On weekends he joined his father in Paris. John was a stern tutor with a warm heart. He spent many hours tutoring his son in the Latin translations of Cicero and Tully's *Orations.*

John also gave his son a blank book in which to write down his observations and feelings about daily events and people. Keeping a journal, or diary, served a purpose. By rereading one's journal, one could see and reflect on how God's Providence, or the "journey" God has designated to a person, continued to influence one's life. The word *journal* comes from *journey.* In addition to the journal's religious merit, it was, John believed, a valuable reference for future generations. John Adams was already consciously aware of the fact that he and his family were making history, and would probably continue to do so in the future. Therefore, he encouraged all the Adams family members to save their journals and letters so that historians could later examine their contents. On January 12, 1779, at the age of eleven, Johnny began his journal. The first entry reads: "A Journal By Me JQA."

Although a strict tutor, John Adams understood that life consisted of much more than studies. He wanted his son to know that fun and exercise were equally important. He made sure to share many lighter moments with Johnny. Together father and son strolled the countryside and attended ballets, musical concerts, and the theater.

Johnny cherished these tender times. He learned to love, obey, and admire his father.

By May 1779, John had completed his European work. He and Johnny were ready to return home. The Chevalier de la Luzerne, the new ambassador from France to the United States, and his secretary, Barbé-Marbois, joined the Adamses on the sail home aboard the French ship *La Sensible*. Luzerne and Barbé-Marbois proved to be entertaining and stimulating company, and Johnny quickly became a favorite of the two Frenchmen. The French diplomats enjoyed discussing serious topics with the young man. One day Luzerne read aloud Blackstone's *Discourse*, while Johnny corrected the ambassador's pronunciation. Luzerne turned to John and said, "Why your son is a master of his own language, like a professor. He teaches us more than you do. He shows us no mercy and makes us no compliments. We must have Mr. John!"[3] Screened by a thick fog, *La Sensible* cruised quietly past British frigates into Boston Harbor on August 2. After five congenial weeks at sea, the French diplomats and the Adamses parted company in Boston.

Upon his return, family and friends hovered over the widely traveled young man, drilling him for descriptions of the places he had seen and the famous people he had met. Johnny wore his expertly tailored Parisian suit and practiced his French on his family. Nabby questioned him in great detail about the French ladies' fashions. It was a joyous reunion!

On August 19, 1779, John Adams was elected as Braintree's representative to the Massachusetts Constitutional Convention. There he wrote the Massachusetts State constitution. Despite this domestic success, John's stay at home was short-lived. Soon Congress asked him to return to France, where preparations for a peace treaty with Great Britain over the revolutionary war were about to begin.

Abigail wept as she bade farewell again to John, Johnny, and this time nine-year-old Charles as they boarded *La Sensible* again on November 13, 1779. As they had agreed the last time, Abigail and John felt the trip overseas would broaden their sons' education and prepare them for their roles in the world. Both Adamses believed God had a predestined purpose for their family. John Thaxter, a private secretary, and Francis Dana, a secretary to the American commission in France, accompanied John and his two sons. Near the end of the voyage, the ship sailed into an Atlantic winter storm, causing it to spring a leak. The captain decided to bring *La Sensible* to a port in Spain for repairs before going on to France.

John was impatient and did not want to wait, so he decided to travel by land across the Pyrenees Mountains into France. Traveling by mule, horseback, and carriages, Adams's group encountered bad roads, impassable winding snowcapped mountains, and crumbling ledges. The group lodged in inns with unkempt rooms and dirt floors. Everyone caught cold. After six long weeks, the weary travelers finally arrived in Paris on February 9.

Johnny wrote a letter to his mother, describing their treacherous journey. Abigail wrote back, reminding Johnny that it was God's Providence that had allowed him to survive the long, dangerous trip. He needed to think about why he'd been placed on earth. She said, "If you have a due sense of your preservation, your next

an assistant with good penmanship. Johnny's schooling at the University of Leyden, although brief, had helped him develop a neat and orderly style of handwriting. This was an important skill in a time when all documents and letters were handwritten.

The two-thousand-mile carriage ride from the Dutch Republic to St. Petersburg, Russia, was long and tedious. Dana and Johnny's work seemed equally endless and boring. For over a year, Dana waited to meet the Russian empress, Catherine the Great. Dana was hoping the empress would recognize America as an independent nation. With no official duties to carry out, Johnny kept up his studies with Dana as his tutor. He also wrote in his journal about the frigid weather and started a lifelong hobby of visiting bookstores.

While Johnny was in Russia, his father, still serving as minister to the Dutch Republic, contracted a high fever. For five days John remained in a coma. Recovery from the illness was very slow. John's spirits rose when he received news that Great Britain had finally surrendered to America. On October 19, 1781, America's general George Washington accepted a formal surrender from the British general, Charles Cornwallis, in Yorktown, Virginia. Negotiations to agree on a peace treaty between America and Great Britain resumed. John would once again be needed in Paris, to assist in the negotiations.

John Thaxter, John's secretary, was returning to America. John would need a new secretary, so he called his son back from Russia. Johnny left Russia on October 30, 1782, in the company of an Italian friend, Count Greco. Passing through the country first by sled, then by boat over the Baltic Sea, Johnny observed, in a letter to his mother,

"The nation is wholly composed of nobles and serfs, or, in other words, of masters and slaves. The countryman is attached to the land in which he is born. . . . This form of government is disadvantageous to the sovereign [ruler], to the nobles and to the people."[6]

The frigid six-month journey from Russia to France took Johnny through Sweden, Denmark, and Prussia. Johnny enjoyed his travels throughout these foreign lands and made warm and lighthearted journal entries during this period. He wrote about the weather, the people he met, and the coffeehouses where he warmed up. In a letter to his mother, Johnny praised Sweden's open hospitality to strangers. He wrote: "Sweden is the country in Europe which pleases me the most, that is, of those I have seen, because their manners resemble more those of my own country than I have seen."[7]

Not quite sixteen, Johnny took his time traveling throughout Europe. He enjoyed being carefree and seeing the sights. Finally, on April 21, 1783, he caught up with his very worried father in the Dutch Republic. John had been wondering just why his wandering son was taking so long to reach him. Johnny blamed the stormy weather for his lengthy

*John Quincy Adams at the age of sixteen.*

journey rather than admit to his father that he had been sightseeing.

The reunion was happy but brief. John was needed in Paris to resume the treaty negotiations. For the next few months, Johnny continued his studies with a private tutor at the Dutch capital, The Hague. However, when negotiations on the treaty came close to being finalized in Paris, John summoned his son to France. There on September 3, 1783, the Treaty of Paris between Great Britain and America was signed. This peace treaty officially declared America's independence. As John's secretary, Johnny was permitted to hand-copy more than a few of the historic peace documents.

Soon after signing the historic treaty, John Adams became the ambassador to Great Britain and went to London with Johnny. Abigail and Nabby joined their family in London, while Charles and Thomas Boylston remained with family members in Massachusetts. At first Abigail did not recognize her son, whom she had not seen for three years, but then she recognized his blue eyes. Johnny was now a young man of sixteen. The family reunion was short-lived, however. While John, Abigail, and Nabby remained in Great Britain, Johnny left Europe's cultural charm and returned to America to further his education.

# 4

# CHANGES

R eturning to the United States meant many changes for Johnny. The first was to receive an American education. His parents wanted Johnny to apply to Harvard College, where his father had been educated. John felt confident that because of Johnny's unique European education, his son would be admitted as a third-year student. However, John was sorely mistaken. Johnny's European experience may have impressed his family and friends, but his lessons abroad had not adequately prepared him for advanced admission to Harvard College. After being tested in geography, mathematics, logic, and foreign language interpretations of literature, Harvard's faculty noted that Johnny was deficient in both Greek and Latin languages. He would need tutoring to gain advanced admission to Harvard.

Reverend John Shaw, Johnny's uncle, became his

tutor. Having to study ten hours a day combined with his uncle's strict methods made Johnny anxious. He became thin and began suffering from "sore eyes." However, eventually his hard work paid off after several months of tutoring. On March 15, 1786, Johnny was examined again and admitted to Harvard as a third-year student.

For the first time, Johnny was no longer a child prodigy among adult foreigners. He now faced his American peers. At times, he acted like his college classmates, sleeping late and skipping lectures on pretty days. During this period, he recorded in his journal college pranks he played along with his fellow students, like breaking faculty windows and booing tutors. One day some students wanted to party on Bunker Hill. They invited John Quincy, as he now called himself, but he refused to join his friends. He remembered the battle he had witnessed as a child. For John Quincy, Bunker Hill would never be a place for revelry but a scene of solemn remembrance.

Harvard was not all fun and pranks. The students there studied hard and participated in debates and exhibitions. John Quincy was a serious student and always put forth his best effort when assigned a difficult topic. He was highly competitive and always tried to do better than his classmates on his assignments. This high level of academic achievement gained him admission to Phi Beta Kappa, an honor society.

The final assignment for all the graduates was a commencement address. Each graduate was given a different subject to write and speak about at the graduation ceremony. John Quincy's subject was "Upon the importance and necessity of public faith to the well being of the community." He was nervous about the prospect of addressing such a large crowd and hoped it would rain, thus forcing the large gathering into smaller, private ceremonies. In his journal the nervous graduate prayed, "O Lord! O Lord! I hope it will rain hard that all their white wigs may be wet that would not let us have a private commencement."[1] Harvard's Commencement Day was July 16, 1787, and the sun shone brightly, so there was an outdoor ceremony on the lawns of the college. John Quincy gave his speech, which was then followed by a family feast prepared by Aunt Mary Cranch, whose son, Billy, had also graduated.

John and Abigail were in Europe and unable to attend their son's commencement, but that did not stop them from looking after their son. Assuming that John Quincy would want to go on to be a lawyer, as he himself had done, John Adams wrote a letter and arranged an apprenticeship for his son under the supervision of Theophilus Parsons, a lawyer in Newburyport, Massachusetts. Along with several other young men, John Quincy began to study law with Parsons. To be admitted to practice law, each pupil had to apprentice for three years and pay a fee to his teacher.

John Quincy was skeptical about his new career. Gone was the intellectual and cultural ambiance that he had relished in Europe and at Harvard College. Now John Quincy had to earn his own salary, a change that frightened him. To make matters worse, law had become a crowded profession—work was scarce, and there was little money to go around.

Secretly, John Quincy also wondered if he could ever be as successful as his father. He was a perfectionist and an overachiever. With his intense competitiveness, John Quincy found it difficult not to constantly compare himself with his famous father, always trying to equal or exceed his father's accomplishments. All this worrying caused John Quincy to experience bouts of dizzy spells, difficulty sleeping, and an overall depression, a mental health condition that causes an individual to feel unhappy. Parsons suggested that he take a vacation, so John Quincy returned home to Braintree.

John and Abigail Adams had returned from Europe. They worried about their son's precarious mental health and visible unhappiness. Under his parents' supervision, John Quincy began to take medicine and exercise frequently. He rode his horse, went ice-skating, and hunted quail. He also forced himself to attend some social activities and to try and enjoy life a little more.

In 1789, George Washington became the first president of the United States, having received the most electoral votes. John Adams had the second most electoral votes, so he became the first vice-president. John Quincy returned to Newburyport to complete his law apprenticeship with Theophilus Parsons when his father took this new, prestigious position in Philadelphia, Pennsylvania, the federal capital at that time.

Despite continuing bouts of depression, John Quincy tried to listen to his parents, who urged him to continue to socialize. He joined a men's social club and attended dinners, summer sailing parties, and winter sleigh rides. He also wrote poems about the women he dated.

One sixteen-year-old girl, Mary Frazier, captured John Quincy's heart. This poem, entitled "A Vision," described her beauty:

*John and Abigail Smith Adams passed on to their son John Quincy
their intense devotion to public service.*

> The roses' colours in her cheeks to blend,
> While Venus added, to complete the fair,
> The eyes blue languish and the golden hair . . . [2]

The twenty-two-year-old law apprentice was in love.
How and when the two met will always be a mystery. John
Quincy kept his relationship with Mary private, even in his
diary. Given the traditional dating practices of the late
eighteenth century, the two probably courted in public.
Usually dates were in someone's home or at a group event.
Eventually, John Quincy wrote to his parents about his
love. Abigail wrote back, reminding her son that he was
not yet financially secure enough to support a wife. When
Mary pressed him for a marriage commitment, the brokenhearted John Quincy obeyed his mother's advice and
ended the relationship.

After completing his three-year apprenticeship, John

Quincy Adams was admitted to practice law in the state of Massachusetts on July 15, 1790. He opened a law office in Boston, but business filtered in very slowly. To fill up his leisure time, he attended card parties, read, and wrote a series of essays in newspapers.

Between June 8 and July 27, 1791, Boston's newspaper, the *Columbian Centinel,* published eleven essays written by John Quincy Adams. These essays were all signed with the name *Publicola,* which is Latin for "friend of the people." On the surface, the *Publicola* essays were critiques of Thomas Paine's article "The Rights of Man." Paine believed that the British people needed to overthrow their monarchy and form a new government, just as the French were currently doing in their country. John Quincy argued that the dynamics of group behavior were responsible for causing the French Revolution. He warned his readers that a country should replace its government using principles of reason, not the dictates of group passion.

John Quincy also had a secret agenda for the *Publicola* essays. This purpose was to defend his father against attacks by Secretary of State Thomas Jefferson. That is why John Quincy had chosen to write using a pseudonym, or pen name. No one would take his writings seriously if they knew the writer was the son of the vice-president. In thirty-two installments in the *Gazette of the United States,* John Adams's essays called the *Discourses of Dalvia* had questioned the wisdom of the French revolt. The first vice-president believed that a strong government depended upon a system of checks and balances among the branches of government. In John Adams's opinion, the French had failed to incorporate this concept into their revolution. Jefferson had interpreted these Adams essays as criticism of the American Revolution. Like many other Americans, Jefferson supported the ongoing French Revolution and compared it to his own country's. Patriots like Jefferson supported the idea of a common people rising up to overthrow a monarchy and replacing it with a new democratic form of government.

After the *Publicola* articles, John Quincy continued to write and debate political issues of his time. Under the pseudonym of a Roman general, "Marcellus," John Quincy wrote a series of articles supporting President George Washington's position of American neutrality in the new war that was being fought between Great Britain and France. In 1793, France's king Louis XVI was tried and executed for treason. Great Britain, Spain, and the Dutch Republic joined an alliance and declared war on France. Writing under his Roman pseudonym, John Quincy reminded Americans that they should remain neutral and concentrate on refilling the national treasury, which had been depleted by the economic pressures of the revolutionary war. He also warned about how the vast coastline of their new land made America vulnerable to both invasion and privateering from foreign enemies.

As the French-British War raged on, Edmund Genêt, France's charismatic ambassador to America, requested that America send to the French some equipment they would need to oppose the British Navy. Genêt assumed America would oblige, because France had aided America during America's revolutionary war. When President Washington denied the request, claiming America's navy was too small to be able to give up its equipment, the angry French diplomat demanded that Congress hold a special meeting to consider his request. Washington responded immediately to this challenge of his presidential authority by asking France to recall Genêt.

Back in Boston, John Quincy was closely following Genêt's actions. He disapproved of the Frenchman's behavior and demands. Again, he wrote essays to the *Columbian Centinel*. This time, he used the pseudonym "Columbus." The Columbus articles made sure to support Washington's actions, pointing out that, as specified under the Constitution, Americans choose their president to represent them in foreign affairs, among other duties. Columbus described Genêt as a " . . . dangerous enemy to the peace and happiness of my country,"[3] and clearly supported a president's right to require the recall of foreign ambassadors. These published views were highly favored and greatly appreciated by President Washington, who knew the true identity of the writer called Columbus.

On May 29, 1794, President Washington officially recognized his anonymous loyal supporter, nominating John Quincy Adams to his father's old post, that of minister to the Dutch Republic. The president made a wise choice for this appointment. John Quincy had lived in the republic as a boy, spoke the language, understood international law, and was familiar with European customs. The Senate unanimously approved his nomination. John Adams proudly told his son, "You will see Europe at the most interesting period in history."[4]

On September 15, 1794, John Quincy Adams gave up his law practice for the life of a foreign diplomat. His parents and his early years abroad had trained him well.

**5**

# A DIPLOMAT

John Quincy wished he had been consulted first before being appointed as minister to the Dutch Republic. He suspected that his father had had something to do with this sudden new career. Although he was twenty-seven years old, John Quincy was not sure he was mature enough yet to handle such an important responsibility.[1] Reluctantly, he arrived on November 4, 1794, at the Dutch Republic city named The Hague, where America had an embassy. He was not alone. Always looking after their children, John and Abigail Adams had sent Thomas Boylston, John Quincy's youngest brother, to accompany him and to act as a secretary.

When the Adams brothers arrived in The Hague, they learned that William V, king of the Dutch Republic, had fled his country. John Adams had been correct: Europe was indeed in the middle of some fascinating historical developments. The bloody French Revolution had turned from the pursuit of liberty for its citizens to the goal of forming an empire and acquiring more land for France. The French Army invaded parts of Italy, Belgium, and the Dutch Republic. As part of his official duties, John Quincy Adams watched, listened, and reported back to his government at home about the military and political movements of France. He had been instructed to remain a minister so long as the Dutch Republic remained an independent country. Now, with William V gone, John Quincy's position as minister became questionable.

As he waited for instructions regarding his position, John Quincy wrote insightful letters to his father about the European events that were quickly unfolding. He offered the opinion that American trade would suffer under conditions of war, but would prosper under peace. Vice-President Adams sometimes shared his son's letters with President Washington, who was quick to praise John Quincy as "the most valuable public character we have abroad."[2] In one letter to his father, John Quincy wrote, "Above all I wish we may never have any occasion for any political connections with Europe."[3] Several years later, President Washington used similar words in his own farewell address.

In official reports and letters sent home, John Quincy proposed in writing that his government should issue passports for American travelers as proof of their citizenship. He also noted that American businessmen needed more legal power regarding foreign trade. John Quincy's efforts on behalf of businessmen abroad ended abruptly when a governmental letter arrived from America, ordering him to leave for Great Britain to assist on the Jay Treaty. The post of minister in the Dutch Republic would be left to his brother, Thomas Boylston Adams.

John Quincy arrived in London too late. The Jay Treaty, a commercial agreement outlining conditions of trade between America and Great Britain, had already been signed. While waiting for his next assignment, John Quincy took advantage of London's busy social scene. He attended the theater and mingled with other Americans. One of them, Joshua Johnson, was an American general consul, an official appointed to look after his country's citizens and businesses in the foreign city. John Quincy found Johnson's second daughter, Louisa Catherine, very attractive, and he visited the family often. Both John Quincy and Louisa enjoyed reading books and playing music. After four months of courting, the young couple became engaged. At about the same time, John Quincy was summoned back to resume his old post in the Dutch Republic. Louisa wished to marry before he left, but John Quincy did not believe that he could support a wife comfortably on his salary.

Before his departure from London, John Quincy and Louisa were invited to a party. Louisa suggested that he dress more fashionably. Although he had purposely ignored his mother's lifelong attempts to correct his sloppy way of dressing, John Quincy tried to please his fiancée and showed up at the party wearing a well-tailored blue suit. Louisa was so delighted that she complimented her fiancé on the choice of his outfit. Coldly, John Quincy warned his future wife never again to get involved in the issue of his clothing. Louisa, who had been proudly holding his arm, quickly dropped it and left John Quincy's side for the rest of the evening.[4]

On May 5, 1796, John Quincy departed for the Dutch

Republic. He was still engaged to Louisa despite the lovers' quarrel. Louisa was disappointed by John Quincy's departure. She would have to settle for courtship through letters, until President Washington changed John Quincy's post to minister of Portugal thirteen months later.

Finally, John Quincy decided to marry Louisa. His new salary could easily support a wife. So before leaving for Portugal, John Quincy returned to London and married Louisa at the Church of All Hallows on July 26, 1797. John Quincy was thirty years old; Louisa was twenty-two. The Johnson family, a few close friends, and Thomas Boylston attended the ceremony. John Quincy and Louisa spent a long, happy honeymoon in London. All was fine until September 9, when the newlyweds were shocked to discover that Louisa's parents had fled London for America, trying to escape a growing mountain of debts. Angry bill collectors and family servants appeared at the newlyweds' hotel, demanding that the Adamses pay them the money owed by the Johnsons. John Quincy paid someone to handle the family problem, but Louisa was crushed. Her pride was deeply hurt by her family's disgrace.[5]

John and Abigail Adams found out about their son's marriage by reading an announcement in a newspaper. They were not surprised. In his letters home, John Quincy had expressed his intention to marry Louisa. John Adams was delighted with the idea of having a daughter-in-law. However, Abigail, true to her history of trying to control her children's actions, even from afar, seriously questioned her son's choice. Long before the marriage, Abigail had made sure to advise her son against marrying someone who had not been born and brought up in America. Because Louisa had been raised as a lady of the court,

*This oil of Louisa Catherine Johnson Adams was painted in 1801 by Edward Savage.*

Abigail feared that she might never adapt to the rough and backward customs of this strange new country.

John Quincy and Louisa never made it to Portugal. That same year, 1797, John Quincy's father was elected president of the United States. President Adams then reassigned his son's post from Portugal to Prussia (which is today Germany and Poland). By stationing his son in Prussia, John Adams could obtain information on neighboring France.

France was going through many turbulent times. By 1797, the French people had revolted and overthrown France's affluent monarchy. While France struggled with forming a new government, General Napoléon Bonaparte led the French Army into Italy and Austria, defeating both countries. France's empire grew. France was also still fighting Great Britain.

John Quincy accepted his father's assignment. On December 5, 1797, Prussia's new king, Frederick William, and his beautiful young queen, Luise Auguste Wilhelmina Amalie, graciously welcomed the Adamses. For two years John Quincy and the Prussians worked together to formulate a commercial treaty. John Quincy's patience, his fluency in the German language, and his organizational skills pleased the Prussians. A close friendship between John Quincy and his Prussian colleagues grew. On his thirty-second birthday, July 11, 1799, the Prussian-American Treaty was signed. The treaty specified which goods could be traded freely between nations and which goods would be unlawful.

While work preoccupied the days, the evenings in Prussia were filled with lavish entertainment. Important state dinners, lively dances, and a card game called whist occupied the upper classes. Louisa frequently suffered from fevers, fainting spells, and several miscarriages, all of which caused her to miss appearances at the royal court.

During her illnesses, the queen and some of the Prussian princesses, who took a special liking to Louisa, helped care for her. Louisa appreciated their kindness, but on one occasion the good intentions of the queen caused a tiff between Louisa and her husband. Because Louisa seemed so pale one evening, the queen presented her with a box of rouge to perk up her color. Before that evening's party, Louisa delightedly applied the reddish makeup to her cheeks. When John Quincy spotted the rouge, he grabbed a towel and scrubbed the makeup off his wife's face, much to her objections. Louisa went to the party without makeup. However, later she learned to stand up to her husband and wore rouge at all social events.

John Quincy was worried about his wife's repeated illnesses. He thought a vacation might improve her health and spirits. Therefore, during the summer of 1800, John Quincy arranged a trip through the southeastern part of Prussia called Silesia, which is part of Poland today. The region was noted for its beautiful mountains and the manufacture of glass and linen. A tour guide took the hikers to the top of lofty mountains, where their eyes gazed out over valleys, villages, pastures, and square-shaped cities. John Quincy took the opportunity to investigate the region for possible trade opportunities between Prussia and America. After two months, the trip was over. Louisa never fully recovered from her illnesses, but their letters to family members indicate that the couple enjoyed themselves away from the political world.

Meanwhile, Napoléon continued to expand France's empire. When the general heard how France's new government had been poorly managed, he decided to return home. The French people were glad to have Napoléon back in France. They thought he brought their country good luck. By popular demand, Napoléon Bonaparte became France's first consul and dictator. In the fall, he increased France's empire by purchasing the Louisiana Territory in North America.

*The part of Prussia called Silesia, which became a peaceful vacation spot for John Quincy and Louisa Adams in the summer of 1800, is shown in this painting.*

From Prussia, John Quincy had plenty to report, but his position as minister was about to end. Back in the United States, Thomas Jefferson won the presidential election of 1800, putting John Adams out of office. Adams took the loss of the presidency hard. He felt that he had personally let his country down. He was also mourning the death of his second son, Charles, who had died from complications of alcoholism. Brokenhearted by these events, John Adams recalled his eldest son from Prussia before his term had ended. However, John Quincy's departure to America was delayed by a happy event. Louisa gave birth to the couple's first son on April 12, 1801, in Prussia. George Washington Adams was named after America's first president, who had recently died in December 1800. Louisa had undergone a difficult childbirth. For many weeks afterward she could not walk. Finally, in mid-June, John Quincy, baby George, and a still weak Louisa Adams sailed to the United States. This would be Louisa's first glimpse of her new country and her first encounter with her in-laws.

# 6

# SENATOR ADAMS

**J**ust as Louisa had feared most, her in-laws' first impression was a disaster! John Quincy had not been home for seven years when, on November 24, 1801, he introduced his new wife and baby to his parents. Louisa was still thin and pale from the strenuous childbirth and from the long ocean journey. Worse, she was suffering from a terrible cold and could barely speak. This made conversation difficult. Baby George was sickly, too. He smelled bad from a constant case of diarrhea. Louisa's frail body worried John and Abigail. Privately, they were concerned about the length of their daughter-in-law's life span. Moreover, Abigail complained that her daughter-in-law had failed to show proper respect to her husband by naming her new grandson after George Washington. Surely, the baby should have been called John Adams II, instead.

Meeting the in-laws was not the only problem for

Louisa. Her mother-in-law had been right! Life in the United States was a difficult adjustment for a foreigner. Describing her first visit to John Quincy's hometown, Louisa later wrote: "Had I step[p]ed into Noah's Ark I do not think I could have been more utterly astonished."[1] Life in early America contrasted sharply with her days in Europe. Louisa was used to European cities, grand cathedrals, and being treated as a lady of the court. In the United States in the early 1800s, she saw mostly farmland,

## SOURCE DOCUMENT

FRONT

THE FARMER's WIFE

or

THE COMPLETE

### COUNTRY HOUSEWIFE.

CONTAINING

Full and ample Directions for the Breeding and Management of Turkies, Fowls, Geese, Ducks, Pigeons, &c.
Instructions for fattening Hogs, pickling of Pork, and curing of Bacon.
How to make Sausages, Hogs-Puddings, &c.
Full Instructions for making Wines from various Kinds of English Fruits, and from Smyrna Raisins.
The Method of making Cyder, Perry, Mead, Mum, Cherry-Brandy, &c.
Directions respecting the Dairy, containing the best Way of making Butter, and likewise Gloucestershire, Chesshire, Stilton, Sage, and Cream Cheese.
How to pickle common English Fruits and Vegetables, with other useful Receipts for the Country House-Keeper.
Full Instructions how to brew Beer and Ale, of all the various Kinds made in this Kingdom.
Ample Directions respecting the Management of Bees, with an Account of the Use of Honey.

To which is added

The Art of Breeding and Managing Song Birds:
Likewise a Variety of Receipts in Cookery,
And other Particulars, well worthy the Attention of Women of all Ranks residing in the Country.

*Instructions, full and plain, we give,*
*To teach the Farmer's Wife,*
*With Satisfaction, how to live*
*The happy Country Life.*

LONDON,

Printed for Alex. Hogg, in Pater-noster Row.

(Price One Shilling and Six-pence.)

To tend the Dairy, and the Poultry rear;
Bake, Brew, and hive the Bees in seasons fair;
Taught by our Work, the Housewife learns with ease,
And while she learns still finds her Stock increase:

*A manual for rural women called the* Complete Country Housewife *was first published in London around 1770. Many settlers brought it with them to the colonies. The book contained instructions on how to raise livestock, prepare meats, grow and preserve fruits and vegetables, and brew ale and beer.*

small homes, dirt roads, and country churches. The plain dress and the early dinner hour shocked Louisa. But what bothered her most was the life of the women. American women spent their days caring for and feeding their children and husbands. At home in London, servants took care of these tasks. Louisa thought the American women were only "a little better off than the Indian squaws. . . ."[2]

In December 1801, John Quincy renewed his law practice and moved his family to a home at 39 Hanover Square in Boston. For the first time, Louisa tried to manage a real household. The work involved in this endeavor kept her unhappy. Discomfort in her new surroundings and her mother-in-law's high expectations made her tense. To make matters worse, John Quincy was quick to criticize his wife for her extravagant expenditures.[3]

While Louisa struggled with domestic life, John Quincy decided to go into politics. At the age of thirty-five, he campaigned for state senator from Suffolk County, Massachusetts. He won on April 5, 1802. He had served for only about a year and was just beginning to gain experience in politics when both United States senators from Massachusetts decided to resign their office. (Prior to the passage of the Seventeenth Amendment to the Constitution in 1913, United States senators were chosen by their state legislatures.) On February 8, 1803, the Massachusetts state legislature elected John Quincy Adams as their United States senator.

Louisa was delighted to move to Washington, D.C. She would be reunited with her mother and sisters, who lived there, and she would also be able to escape the constant surveillance of her opinionated mother-in-law. John and Abigail Adams were proud of their son's accomplishment.

Abigail continued to give John Quincy unsolicited advice on his wardrobe; in particular, she suggested that he buy a new coat so as to look the part of a well-respected senator.

Just before the move to Washington, the couple celebrated a joyful event: the birth of a second son. It was on Independence Day, July 4, 1803, and the new baby was born just as the first guns were fired to mark the special event. Much to John and Abigail's pleasure, this baby was named John Adams II after his grandfather.

The twenty-day sailing trip from Boston to Washington was troublesome. The Adamses encountered stormy weather. Everyone was seasick, and two-year-old George playfully tossed the keys to his parents' trunks overboard.

On October 20, 1803 John Quincy and Louisa arrived in the three-year-old federal capital. Washington, D.C., was a swampy, mosquito-infested village. Small homes and boardinghouses lined the muddy streets. Protestant churches had not yet been built, so nondenominational services were held in the Capitol and the Treasury Building. Most members of Congress shared shabby rooms in boardinghouses, while their wives remained back in their home states. The Adams family was an exception. They remained together, boarding in the home of Nancy Hellen, Louisa's sister, which was just a three-mile walk from the Capitol.

Senator Adams arrived in Washington too late to vote on the Louisiana Territory purchase. France, in desperate need of money to fight Great Britain, decided to sell its Louisiana Territory to the United States. President Thomas Jefferson authorized the purchase, fearing that if the French continued to hold the territory, the Mississippi River might be closed to American trade.

Both parts of Congress—the Senate and the House of Representatives—passed legislation authorizing the purchase. This act angered the Federalists, a political party that favored a strong federal government. The Federalists considered the Louisiana Purchase unconstitutional. In fact, the Constitution did not specifically grant the president the power to make such a purchase. John Quincy Adams, who belonged to the Federalist party, agreed with the actions of Jefferson, a Democratic-Republican, even though he arrived in Washington too late to vote. He believed that the purchase was in the best interest of the country. The Federalists were appalled when John Quincy crossed party lines to support Jefferson. They were even more aggravated when John Quincy proposed an amendment to the Constitution authorizing the acquisition of territories. The amendment did not pass. Nevertheless, legislation authorizing the Louisiana Purchase was passed on April 30, 1803.

Congress always recessed in the spring and resumed its sessions in the fall. During recess, members of Congress returned to their home states to resume their other professions. The Adams family took their recess at John Quincy's childhood home in Braintree.

In 1805, Harvard College elected John Quincy the Boylston Professor of Rhetoric and Oratory, a benefaction bestowed on him by Nicholas Boylston, a cousin of John Quincy's paternal grandmother. For half the year, the new professor lectured twice a week to students at the university on current political issues. The position delighted John Quincy, because it challenged his intellect.

That summer Abigail Adams proposed that her two young grandsons, George and John II, would receive a better education in Massachusetts than in the primitive city of Washington, D.C., and she invited the boys to live with her and their grandfather. This suggestion by her meddling mother-in-law upset Louisa. She loved her sons dearly and wanted them to remain with her in Washington while Congress was in session. However, an event changed Louisa's mind. On Christmas Day in 1805, a group of Cherokees boldly entered the Hellen boardinghouse and refused to leave. Louisa and a few other women were alone. Not knowing how to get rid of the uninvited guests, Louisa decided to entertain them by playing the piano. After completing her performance, Louisa realized the Cherokees were still planning to stay. Finally Louisa, thinking quickly, handed the intruders some ribbons, hoping that a present would inspire them to leave. Indeed, satisfied with the gifts, the Cherokees left. After this brush with potential danger, the Adamses agreed that their boys might be better off in Massachusetts.

During the 1806 summer recess, Boston experienced a total eclipse of the sun. John Quincy went to a friend's garden to witness the once-in-a-lifetime event. Wearing special glasses to shield his eyes, he gazed at the eclipse. For four and one-half minutes the sun's face was completely covered. Using a lantern to read the thermometer, he noted that the temperature had dropped eleven degrees during the event. John Quincy was now hooked on astronomy.

When November came, Senator Adams returned to Washington, where he continued to dissatisfy the Federalist party. Always a man of principle, he supported bills that he believed would help all of the United States. In his own words, he was "a man of my whole country."[4] This view did not please the Federalists, whose interests were often not shared by the senator. One such interest became apparent in 1807. It regarded the *Chesapeake-Leopard* affair.

The *Leopard* was a frigate in Great Britain's Royal Navy. One day, on the high seas, it signaled the American frigate, the U.S.S. *Chesapeake*. Thinking that the British wanted to board the *Chesapeake* to drop off mail headed to Europe, the American ship turned around. It was a common courtesy of that time for American and British ships to deliver each other's mail. However, instead of sending mail, the British wanted to search the *Chesapeake* to see if any deserters from the British Navy were on board. Many British sailors resented the severe treatment they were receiving in the British Navy, and some had deserted, stowing away on American merchant or navy ships. When the commander of the *Chesapeake* refused to let the British search his ship, the *Leopard*'s cannons fired three shots into the *Chesapeake*'s broadside. Twenty-one Americans were injured in the blast.

Americans were outraged. President Jefferson did not want to start a war, because the American military defense was unprepared. Instead, he asked Congress to pass the Embargo Act, prohibiting American trade ships from leaving port to go to any foreign country. The act also forbade imported goods from arriving in the United States. Jefferson believed that the embargo would eventually deprive Great Britain of food and naval supplies necessary to its economy, which were ordinarily supplied by American trade.

Senator Adams supported Jefferson's position, because he thought the embargo would teach the British to respect American rights at sea. His position was extremely unpopular among the Federalists in New England. New

England's economy relied heavily upon trade, and the representatives from New England wanted no legislation that would interfere with its profitable commerce. John Quincy was aware of this regional interest, but he reasoned that the embargo would benefit the country, overall, in the long run. The Embargo Act was passed.

After a year, however, it became clear that the act had backfired. Instead of hurting Great Britain, the embargo had boosted British overseas trade and injured American trade. Adams and Jefferson had been wrong.

In an early election, an angry Massachusetts legislature voted James Lloyd, Jr., to replace Adams in the United States Senate. John Quincy Adams, humiliated, resigned from Congress several months before the end of his term. The only bright spot in his life was the birth of a third son. Named after John Quincy's deceased brother, Charles Francis Adams was born on August 18, 1807.

# 7

# A DIPLOMAT'S EXILE

Once again John Quincy fell into a deep depression. His pride had been severely damaged by losing the election, and he believed he had failed as a public servant. The ex-senator resigned himself to teaching at Harvard and resuming his law practice.

At the age of forty, he clearly believed that his political career was over. How wrong he was. President James Madison, who had succeeded Jefferson, had come to admire John Quincy's insight into political affairs. Madison offered him a position as minister to Russia. Some politicians regarded this as an "honorable exile."[1] The prospect of being exiled from the country that had appeared to reject him tempted John Quincy. He was tired of the Federalists' snubbing him for having supported Jefferson. John Quincy had held two successful diplomatic positions in a foreign country before. Without even consulting his wife, he quickly accepted the Russian post.

Going to Russia meant that Louisa would again be separated from her sons George and John II. Once again, they would remain with their grandparents to continue their education. Two-year-old Charles Francis would go to Russia with his parents. Louisa felt guilty about deserting her two oldest children. She felt that at ages eight and six the boys needed a mother's care and influence.[2] At least while John Quincy had been a senator she could see her sons six months out of the year. Being in Russia meant she would not see them for years. Louisa was angered by this imposition on the family.[3]

Nevertheless, on October 23, 1809, the Adamses arrived in the beautiful city of St. Petersburg. Located on the Baltic Sea, the capital was covered by ice and snow from October until May. The winter offered a long series of glittery court and entertainment events. As had been true in the Prussian court, French was spoken, and extravagantly dressed diplomats and their wives attended long, lavish dinners, plays, concerts, teas, and dances. Sometimes the diplomats' children were invited, too. Once there was a costume party, where Charles Francis received applause for his American Indian costume. Evenings often ended with supper served at 1:00 A.M.

John Quincy found this elaborate routine most irregular. Such strenuous nightlife interfered with his morning ritual of reading the Bible in either French or German, followed by a long, brisk walk of one hundred twenty steps per minute.[4] He also disapproved of Russia's lavish lifestyle. His meager minister's salary would hardly support the big house and numerous Russian servants assigned to his family. To solve this problem, the thrifty New Englander scouted the city until he found an affordable alternative. Instead of keeping his assigned servants, who John Quincy also discovered were stealing from him, he arranged with a local restaurant to supply the family's meals.

John Quincy wrote to his mother, complaining about Russia's extravagant lifestyle. Abigail interpreted her son's letter as a plea to return home. She took it upon herself to write to President James Madison asking for her son's immediate recall during the summer of 1810. When Justice William Cushing of the United States Supreme Court died in September, Madison obliged Abigail Adams's request by assigning John Quincy to become a United States Supreme Court judge. When he heard the news nearly a year later, due the slowness of the mail, John Quincy was furious that his mother had intervened. He was heavily involved in his work as minister to Russia. On June 3, 1811, he wrote to Madison declining the position, explaining that he preferred diplomacy to law. He was also concerned about Louisa's delicate new pregnancy. He felt the long trip home might cause her to lose the baby.

John Quincy's mission as a foreign minister was to develop a friendship with the Russian czar, or leader, so as to cultivate both trade and a maritime treaty between Russia and the United States. With John Quincy's stiff, intellectual nature, casual socializing was usually a difficult task. Fortunately, friendship with the czar came easily. Often John Quincy encountered thirty-year-old Czar Alexander I on his morning outings. Together they walked and chatted about whatever subject happened to be on their minds. Sometimes it was politics, sometimes it was trivial matters, like the merits of flannel underwear.

These informal meetings grew into a strong, trusting relationship.

In 1811, when Louisa gave birth to a daughter, Louisa Catherine, the czar claimed the infant as his godchild. Sadly, the baby died from acute dysentery before her first birthday. As the distraught parents grieved over their baby daughter's death, they received more terrible news. A package of letters arrived reporting that Louisa's mother had died from a high fever, and that John Quincy's sister, Nabby, was dying from breast cancer. Unfortunate news from home did not help alleviate John Quincy's recurring bouts of depression and insomnia.

By the spring of 1812, however, personal problems gave way to global concerns. Russia and France were preparing to go to war. Napoléon's plan for controlling all of Europe included Russia. The czar shared his fear of the French dictator with his American friend. While John

Quincy awaited Russia's inevitable war, he learned that the United States and Great Britain were also heading toward war. Great Britain was refusing to grant American ships maritime neutrality rights. The British Navy stopped and

*Nabby Adams, John Quincy's older sister, is shown here in an oil portrait done in 1785 by Mather Brown. Nabby died of breast cancer.*

searched American ships and impressed, or forced, American seamen into their navy. The British were still at war with Napoléon and France, and they desperately needed seamen. The impressment of American sailors caused Congress to declare war on Great Britain on June 18, 1812. A few months later, Russia was at war with France. Napoléon managed to raise a gigantic army of Italians, Poles, Swiss, Dutch, German, and Spanish troops to invade Russia.

The War of 1812, as it became known, put Czar Alexander I in a delicate position, because Russia was friendly with both Great Britain and the United States. Russia did not wish to offend the British since both Russia and Great Britain were united in war against France, trying to repress Napoléon's expanding empire. To appear neutral and help resolve the problem, Alexander offered that his prime minister, Count Romantzoff, could mediate between Great Britain and the United States. President Madison accepted the Russian's offer, but Great Britain declined. Instead, Great Britain requested direct negotiations with American representatives.

While the czar was trying to find a way to help the United States and Great Britain resolve their problems, Napoléon's enormous army marched deeper into Russia. So greatly were they outnumbered by Napoleon's troops that the Russian Army avoided battles again and again. However, just one month after its initial invasion, Napoléon's army ran out of food and shelter. Napoléon ordered his troops to return to France. As they trudged homeward, the army became weak from hunger, and then disaster struck. Winter had arrived. Daily snowstorms bombarded the starving troops. Thousands died from

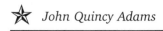

*French dictator and general Napoléon Bonaparte, shown here on horseback, planned to extend his empire to control all of Europe.*

starvation and exposure to frigid temperatures. Napoléon's dream of capturing Russia was failing. In 1813, Prussia, Austria, and Sweden would join Great Britain and Russia and declare war on France. On March 21, 1814, the allied countries captured Paris and forced Napoléon to give up his throne. Napoléon was then sent away, or exiled, to Elba, an island off the coast of Italy. France brought back their king, Louis XVII.

Soon after Napoléon's exile, John Quincy received a new assignment. He was to travel to Ghent, Flanders (Belgium today), to negotiate a treaty in an effort to end the War of 1812. He decided to leave Louisa and Charles Francis in St. Petersburg. On August 8, 1814, John Quincy met the other four United States representatives—Albert

Gallatin, James Bayard, Henry Clay, and Jonathan Russell. The British representatives in Ghent were Admiral Lord Gambier, Dr. William Adams, and Henry Goulburn.

Negotiations began. The British representatives never mentioned either the lack of American maritime neutrality rights or the impressment of American seamen into the British Navy, the reasons for the War of 1812. Instead, they demanded that a change be made in the boundary between the United States and Canada, a British territory. The British also requested a separate state for American Indians, and that the United States give up fishing rights off the coast of Newfoundland and Labrador, Canada. After listening to these ridiculous demands by the British, John Quincy believed further negotiations would be hopeless.

The other American representatives disagreed with John Quincy, however, and so day after day, the negotiations continued. The Americans met in the afternoon for two hours; then they dined. Each note written on the negotiations had to be reviewed by the British government in London, and this process took weeks. Between notes, the American representatives entertained themselves. John Quincy was dismayed by their behavior: "They sit after dinner and drink bad wine and smoke cigars, which neither suits my habits nor my health, and absorbs time which I cannot spare," he wrote in his diary.[5] In another entry, John Quincy complained about fellow delegate Henry Clay's all-night card parties: Just before rising, he said, "I hear Clay's company retiring from his chamber."[6]

While the other representatives enjoyed themselves, John Quincy maintained his strict routine. He rose early in the morning, walked, and wrote. He distanced himself from the others by eating alone. Finally, Clay confronted

John Quincy about this social offense, explaining that the other delegates felt Adams's solitary behavior was rude. He invited John Quincy to eat with the other delegates. Reluctantly, John Quincy accepted Clay's invitation and dined with the group. Eventually, a deep, lifelong friendship blossomed between the two representatives.

Henry Clay was an unlikely friend for the conservative John Quincy. In fact, the two men were opposites in almost every way. The tall, lanky speaker of the House of Representatives was a highly ambitious politician and a southern slave owner. He also had a reputation as a gambler, a drinker, and a womanizer. Despite these vices, Clay possessed a charismatic personality that charmed even the dour New Englander. In a letter to Louisa, John Quincy admitted that Clay was the "friendliest man in the world."[7]

However, at the negotiating table, John Quincy and Clay often clashed. So intense were their disagreements that negotiators thought they were personal enemies. Often they carried on explosive arguments and exchanged foul language. John Quincy fought to keep America's fishing rights

*Henry Clay, a southerner and slaveowner, was known for his drinking, card-playing, and late-night parties. Despite the fact that John Quincy Adams, a proper gentleman from New England, disapproved of Clay's social behavior, the two men became good friends.*

along the Canadian coast and correspondingly to grant the British navigational rights on the Mississippi River. Clay, on the other hand, opposed granting Great Britain navigational rights on the Mississippi but agreed to forfeit American fishing rights. Tempers flared as each protected his home state's interests. Eventually, Clay approached his friend. He explained that the British were playing brag, a card game like poker, with the Americans. John Quincy did not know how to play brag. Clay explained that to win at the game, one must pretend to be confident about his hand of cards and outbrag the opponent. Clay thought it was time to play brag with the British. Once he understood the game, John Quincy agreed.[8]

For ten days in November 1814, the Americans wrote and then rewrote the terms of the agreement to the War of 1812. Then, "playing brag," the Americans handed the British their treaty conditions. This time the British seriously examined the American demands. The British had been stalling at a negotiation settlement, because they had been winning the war. Now, however, the Americans were winning. Great Britain had been engaged in two wars, first with France and then with the United States. Fighting two wars had taken its toll in British taxes and manpower. The British needed to end their war with the United States. Peace was in sight.

John Quincy convinced everyone that the terms of the treaty must be based on prewar conditions: Issues like fishing rights and boundaries were to revert to the way things were before the war started. The issue of impressment of seamen was totally omitted, since the practice had already ended with Napoléon's exile. The British no longer needed sailors to fight France. On Christmas Eve, 1814,

Great Britain and the United States signed the Treaty of Ghent, formally ending the friction between the two nations. John Quincy wrote in his diary, "I cannot close the record of this day without an humble offering to God . . . for peace at this place . . . and the union of my country."[9]

After the treaty was signed, John Quincy visited Paris while waiting for his new assignment. He wrote to Louisa asking her to join him. Before Louisa left for Paris, a Russian countess strongly insisted upon reading her fortune. The countess told Louisa that halfway through her trip she would have to change her travel plans. Someone of great character would cause confusion in Europe, and this chaos would make her traveling difficult. However, the countess reassured Louisa that eventually she would be joyfully reunited with her husband. With this serious forewarning, Louisa, seven-year-old Charles, a French nurse, and two armed servants left Russia on February 12, 1815.

During the long trip by sled, the cold weather in Russia froze their food. Arriving in Prussia, they switched from sleds to wheeled carriages. Louisa was delighted to meet with old friends along the way. When her journey was half over, the countess's prophecy came true. Louisa's carriage hobbled over a battlefield that had borne witness to the war against Napoléon. Scattered uniforms, boots, caps, and the bones of ten thousand men littered the fields. The sight and smell of the dead made Louisa feel faint and sick to her stomach.

Beyond the battlefields, Louisa heard rumors that Napoléon had escaped from the island of Elba and had formed new French troops. He was returning to France to regain his power. Indeed, Louisa encountered a group of French soldiers outside Paris. The soldiers, having seen the

Russian carriage, and assuming that Louisa and her traveling companions must be Russian, shouted that all should be killed. Quickly, Louisa presented her passport to a French general who shouted back to his soldiers that the lady was an American. Waving her handkerchief, Louisa cleverly shouted in French, "Long live, Napoléon!" The general then recommended a place to spend the night and a safe route to Paris for the next morning.

Back in Paris, John Quincy was anxiously waiting for his wife and son. He, too, had witnessed the renewed French support for Napoléon. Rumors were spreading like wildfire that their exiled leader was returning to Paris. Literally overnight, along their wide boulevards, the fickle Parisians replaced pictures of the royal family with pictures of Napoléon. Enthusiastic crowds gathered in the city, hoping to catch a glimpse of their hero. John Quincy mingled among the Parisians so that he, too, could see Napoléon. He never did, but finally, on March 23, 1815, Louisa and Charles Francis arrived safely.

On May 7, John Quincy received his new assignment. It was a position his father had held thirty years earlier. John Quincy had been appointed ambassador to Great Britain. (One day, his third son, Charles Francis Adams, would also become America's ambassador to Great Britain, making three consecutive generations of Adamses who would hold that post.) Both John Quincy and Louisa were delighted with the news. After being apart from their family for six years, the Adams's two oldest sons, George and John II, would be able to join their parents in Great Britain. Louisa could also visit old friends.

For the next two years, the family lived in Ealing, a town outside London. Life was pleasant. Their charming country cottage had fruit trees and a beautiful garden. The rent included a pew at a local Anglican church where the whole family congregated regularly. John Quincy renewed his youthful passion of writing poetry, and he enjoyed leisurely countryside walks, games, kite-flying, and theater outings with his family. For a change, John Quincy felt cheerful and relaxed.

For the most part, John Quincy's workload was light. He greeted Americans, issued passports, and negotiated the terms of navigation rights and commerce with Great Britain. As they had done in Ghent, the team of John Quincy, Gallatin, and Clay often met with British representatives to discuss the commercial and navigational issues. On July 3, 1815, they signed a commercial treaty. This time, however, there was a new twist.

In the past, representatives had affixed their signatures in blocks to commercial treaties. For example, all the British representatives might sign first, followed by all the American representatives. John Quincy believed that this positioning gave the appearance that one country was superior to the other. For this reason, he insisted that the individuals' signatures alternate. For example, one American representative might sign, followed by a British representative, and then followed by another American. He had conceived of this idea after hearing negative criticism about how the signing of the Treaty of Ghent had been handled.

Clay and Gallatin initially objected to this change in signing procedure. However, the British agreed with John Quincy's method. The treaty was signed using the alternating signatures method, and this procedure is still practiced today, supposedly helping to establish equality among nations.

During the autumn, John Quincy accidentally shot off a pistol, which burned his hand and injured his eyes. The eyes became so sore and inflamed that he could not see or sleep. The doctor prescribed placing leeches, or blood-sucking worms, on the eyelids to control the inflammation, a practice that some doctors still prescribe today. Six leeches were applied to the eyelids for an hour, while warm towels were used to absorb the blood the leeches had drawn out. The treatment was unsuccessful, and caused his face to swell for a month. During this time, John Quincy dictated his business requirements to Louisa, and she wrote out letters for her husband. She also read and sang to him during this period of recovery.

After two years in Great Britain, John Adams wrote to John Quincy. He missed his son, and he especially missed his grandsons eating berries and messing up his desk at the Big House in Quincy. John urged his son to return home to his country. So when President-elect James Monroe offered John Quincy Adams the position of secretary of state in the new Cabinet, he gratefully accepted the post. His diplomatic exile was over.

# 8

# SECRETARY OF STATE

After his disastrous experience as a senator, John Quincy felt he had at last redeemed himself in the eyes of his fellow American citizens and his parents. Eight successful and eventful years abroad had passed. As minister to Russia, he had cultivated a lasting friendship with the czar, developed a commercial treaty, and helped write and sign the Treaty of Ghent, ending the War of 1812. His final mission as ambassador to Great Britain had also been highly successful.

After visiting for a month with his parents in Massachusetts, John Quincy and Louisa left for Washington, D.C., where they had bought a home on F Street. Much to Louisa's dismay, her sons once again chose to remain with their grandparents. This time John II and Charles Francis attended the Boston Latin School, while George began Harvard College.

On September 22, 1817, John Quincy Adams was sworn in as secretary of state under President James Monroe. The secretary of state oversees all foreign diplomacy for the United States. John Quincy's experience as a foreign diplomat made him ideally suited to this high Cabinet position. However, he soon discovered that not everyone handled details in the thorough and organized manner he was accustomed to in his own affairs.

James Monroe, now president, had been the previous secretary of state, under President James Madison. Monroe had literally left his unfinished paperwork scattered across his desk when he left the secretary's office. Important letters and translations had been lost or misplaced. John Quincy made it his first priority to organize this mess. He began by indexing and filing all diplomatic papers and records. Louisa continued to assist her husband by copying each private letter in her own hand. Her efforts saved John Quincy, who still suffered from sore eyes, along with a new ailment, a right hand that trembled with palsy, a form of paralysis accompanied by involuntary tremors.

John Quincy also wrote to American ambassadors

## SOURCE DOCUMENT

*The effects of palsy on his right hand are evident here in John Quincy Adams's signature, which shows his shaky handwriting.*

abroad and to foreign representatives living in Washington. In letters to the American ambassadors abroad, he described his own experience as a foreign diplomat. He warned the ambassadors never to accept gifts and to alternate the order of countries' signatures on successive treaties. He also instructed them to report back to him all relevant observations regarding politics, the common people's attitudes, and the economic conditions of their assigned countries. To the foreign representatives stationed in Washington, John Quincy reported that President Monroe would now prefer formal meetings; no longer would casual visits to the president be accepted.

During the winter of 1818, John Quincy began negotiations with Don Luís de Onís, Spain's representative to the United States. The United States wanted to extend the western boundary of the Louisiana Purchase all the way to the Pacific Ocean and also annex Florida, which was owned by Spain. Florida was important to the United States because its rivers provided shipping access to Mississippi, Alabama, and Georgia, making trade quicker and easier.

Besides, Spain had been unwilling or unable to control native Seminole Indian tribe attacks along the border states. Seminole warriors frequently attacked American cities, and then took refuge inside Spanish fortresses in Florida. Secretary of War John C. Calhoun ordered American army troops to the border between Georgia and East Florida to control the attacks. On November 30, 1817, Seminole warriors fatally attacked an American military hospital ship on the Appalachicola River in Georgia. The attack was made in retaliation for American soldiers having burned a Seminole village, killing some villagers. The warriors then fled to Florida for protection.

Afterward, General Andrew Jackson was assigned by President Monroe to stop any further Seminole attacks. Monroe instructed him to pursue the Seminoles into Florida, but not to attack any Spanish fortresses without specific permission from the United States Department of War. General Jackson wrote to Monroe on January 6, 1818, suggesting that the United States take possession of East Florida. Controlling Florida would be a repayment for Spain's neglect in failing to stop Seminole raids. Hearing nothing from the president, Jackson assumed that he had the authority to invade Florida. During April and May, Jackson and three thousand soldiers marched into Florida. The army stopped the Seminoles' attacks, captured three Spanish forts, and tried and executed two British men responsible for encouraging the Seminoles.

Back in Washington, President Monroe was shocked to hear the news about General Jackson's unauthorized invasion. Monroe did not remember receiving Jackson's letter, but he did acknowledge that he had been sick in bed during the time Jackson said he sent the letter. Monroe called his Cabinet to the White House on May 4, 1818, to discuss this serious and embarrassing crisis. Many believed Jackson's attack was unconstitutional, because only Congress had the power to declare war. Some Cabinet members recommended that Jackson be censured, or publicly reprimanded, for his unauthorized invasion. Only John Quincy Adams defended the general. He classified Jackson's military decision as an act of self-defense against the Seminoles, a hostile enemy. There was much heated discussion among the Cabinet members and congressmen about whether or not to censure Jackson, but in the end, John Quincy's powerful arguments prevailed, and Jackson was not censured.

In his role as secretary of state, John Quincy now needed to convince Spain and Great Britain that Jackson's actions had been justified. Privately in his journal, the secretary of state recognized Jackson's wrongdoing. On his fifty-second birthday, John Quincy called on God to grant him courage and guidance. Beset with insomnia, hand tremors, and the intense Washington summer heat, he worked on his official report to Onís. The report reminded Spain of its obligation to keep peace along the Georgia and Florida border. John Quincy insisted that it was Spain's failure to maintain peace that had forced General Jackson to act in self-defense. The report then stated that President Monroe would return the Spanish forts now under control of Jackson's army to Spanish rule. John Quincy's prayers were answered: Onís accepted his explanation of Jackson's invasion into Florida.

At the same time, John Quincy was also negotiating with Great Britain about the unsettled business from the War of 1812. The Convention of 1818, as the negotiation meeting was called, renewed the United States' rights to fish off the coast of Canada that his father had claimed in the Treaty of Paris in 1783. This treaty had also defined the American-Canadian border along the 49th parallel, giving the Louisiana Purchase a northern boundary.

During the convention, John Quincy received news that his mother, Abigail, had died on October 28, 1818, three days after John and Abigail's fifty-fourth wedding anniversary. The seventy-four-year-old matriarch, whose courage during the American Revolution had made her an outstanding patriot, had died from typhoid fever. John Quincy could not attend the funeral due to the important negotiations between Great Britain and the United States. Although John Quincy had always resented his mother's domineering manner, he told his sons that he admired her lively nature, her love of literature, her unflinching patriot-ism, and her devotion to helping people.[1]

In November, John Quincy was once again in communication with the Spanish government regarding the Florida and Oregon territories. The United States still wanted to acquire these Spanish territories. Secretary of State Adams knew that Spain was struggling to control rebellions in Latin America. Spain, therefore, lacked the military power sufficient to control the Florida and Oregon territories. This was proven by Jackson's invasion. In a written statement, John Quincy reminded Spain of Jackson's military action and demanded that Spain maintain order in its territories or else turn the lands over to the United States. Spain recognized its military inability to control what happened in the territories. Consequently, the Spanish government agreed to relinquish the Florida and Oregon territories in the United States.

On February 22, 1819, John Quincy and Onís signed the Adams-Onís Treaty, which was also called the Transcontinental Treaty. The new southern boundary of the United States now included the Florida peninsula, which continued westward along Texas's Sabine River. What is now modern Texas remained Spanish territory. The Oregon territory spanned the area from Spanish California to Russian Alaska. The northern border of the Oregon territory would have to be negotiated with Great Britain. For the first time, the United States' western boundary extended to the Pacific Ocean. By defending General Andrew Jackson, John Quincy had successfully increased the country's area, provided a pathway to the Pacific Ocean, and cleared the United States of blame for Jackson's unauthorized invasion into Florida. Despite the fact that it would be several years before Congress ratified the treaty, John Quincy regarded the Transcontinental Treaty as the most important work of his life.[2]

In 1817, John Quincy conducted a study and reported to Congress on weights and measurements. The purpose of this study was to recommend a uniform system of weights and measurements for the entire United States. At the time, different parts of the country had different ways of weighing and measuring goods sold for trade. Having one system would unite the country and make trade consistent. John Quincy's background had prepared him well for this assignment. His scientific curiosity and his scholarly and organized nature had helped him study Europe's weight and measurement systems while he was working in Russia.

To begin his study, John Quincy requested that each of the twenty-four states submit its standards on weights and measurements. Slowly, state reports trickled into the secretary of state's office. Many state reports were incomplete or inaccurate, but despite the unimpressive response, John Quincy kept working. Sometimes he would awaken between three and five in the morning just to study different kinds of mathematical and scientific measurements, which fascinated and absorbed him.[3] Louisa commented that her husband's " . . . whole mind is so intent on weights and measures that you would suppose his very existence depended on this subject."[4] Even John Adams pleaded with his son to "throw the weights and measures up in the air," and come home for a vacation.[5]

Family pleas did not lessen John Quincy's dedication to his assignment. Three years later, in February 1821, the Report of the Secretary of State upon Weights and Measures was finally presented to Congress. It was supposed to have been a list of proposed universal tables and measures. Instead, Congress received a lengthy philosophical and historical evaluation of the general subject. For the future, John Quincy recommended using France's metric system, not only for the United States, but for all countries. He envisioned a universal system that would benefit everyone. The report had little influence on Congress, however, and the United States never adopted the metric system. After sending copies of his report to knowledgeable individuals in Europe and the United States, John Quincy resumed dealing with foreign affairs.

By 1821 most of Latin America had fought a revolution against Spanish rule. On March 8, 1822, President Monroe wrote to Congress and asked that Rio de la Plata (Argentina), Colombia, Chile, Peru, and Mexico be recognized as independent countries. Congress approved the recognitions and made money available to appoint American ambassadors to those new countries.

Meanwhile, Great Britain asked the United States to join forces in warning European nations against further colonization in Latin America. John Quincy questioned Britain's motives on this issue. Great Britain's navy dominated the seas and did not need the United States military. It was John Quincy's belief that the United States should warn Europe alone, without any British involvement. He suggested that the United States adopt a policy whereby the Western Hemisphere would remain free from intervention or colonization by any European power. John Quincy strongly believed that America's principles of liberty and self-government were inconsistent with another country's attempts to exert power over American territory and citizens. His noncolonization proposal reflected his belief that Europe and America were separate and different political entities, and thus the Western Hemisphere should be closed to further foreign colonization. President Monroe listened carefully to his secretary of state.

John Quincy wrote a paper for the president, detailing his ideas on foreign policy. Then the president and his

*President James Monroe (standing), wearing old-fashioned knee breeches and stockings, discusses the policy that will later be known as the Monroe Doctrine with his Cabinet. John Quincy Adams, Monroe's secretary of state, is the third man from the left.*

Cabinet revised the secretary of state's thoughts, or as John Quincy later complained, used "the cream of my paper,"[6] or the best parts. On December 2, 1823, President James Monroe delivered his annual message to Congress and to the world. Today's equivalent is the president's annual State of the Union address, although in Monroe's day, the president would write his message, not deliver it orally. It would be left to a clerk in Congress to read the message aloud.

There were four major themes to the president's message:

- The free and independent American countries were not subjects for further colonization.

- The political systems in the Americas are different and separate from Europe's.

- The United States would not interfere in European matters and would respect existing European colonies in the Americas.

- To force European expansion in the Americas would be considered a threat to the security of the United States.

Together these themes later became known as the Monroe Doctrine. At the time, neither President Monroe nor Secretary of State Adams realized they had formulated one of America's basic foreign policies.

Foreign reactions to the Monroe Doctrine were mixed. Shocked European leaders doubted the power of the United States military to enforce its words. Swedish and French liberals applauded. Most Latin American countries found the whole warning unnecessary. They had not expected any European interference in their affairs and saw no need for a warning.[7] Despite these widely mixed reactions, no country challenged the United States' authority. John Quincy's principles formulated in Monroe's message caught the world's attention. For the first time, the United States was viewed as a potential world power.

As secretary of state, John Quincy's efforts had resulted in an increase in the nation's territory from the Mississippi River to the Pacific Ocean. He had helped negotiate an end to conflicts involving the Seminole Indians, Spain, and Great Britain. Through his part in the Monroe Doctrine, he helped make America become a strong, independent world power capable of keeping foreign nations from colonizing its land and its neighbors.

Thus with the end of the Monroe administration drawing near, John Quincy dared to think about the presidency. He hoped that his extraordinary accomplishments as secretary of state would lead him to the Executive Mansion. His parents had prepared him, through their teachings and their example, to better his country through politics. Seeking the highest office in the land would fulfill both God's duty and his parents' dreams. In 1821, John Quincy Adams announced his candidacy. He hoped to add another Adams presidency to the history books.

# 9

# LIKE FATHER, LIKE SON

Since the administration of John Adams, three successive secretaries of state—Jefferson, Madison, and Monroe—had become the next president. John Quincy Adams hoped to continue that trend. Slowly, however, he was coming to realize that his impressive accomplishments as secretary of state might not be enough to win the election of 1824.

The election process was changing. At one time, only men who owned property or paid taxes could vote. Now, most states' election processes allowed any white male over the age of twenty-one to vote. This change in the voting rules required a different approach to campaigning. Now both popularity and an agreeable personality were needed to attract new voters.

John Quincy was now fifty-seven years old. He was a short, bald, stout man and had a shrill voice that cracked when he was agitated. He pictured himself as "a man of reserved, cold, austere [strictly moral], and forbidding manners."[1] John Quincy was acutely aware that as a presidential candidate, he lacked voter appeal. Therefore, with much reluctance, he made an attempt to abandon his cold, scholarly nature and began to socialize.

In 1824 political campaigning was mostly disguised as a series of social events. John Quincy learned to practice his technique. He visited hotels, boardinghouses, and private homes. To boost his popularity, he decided to celebrate the ninth anniversary of the Battle of New Orleans by holding a ball in honor of General Andrew Jackson, the hero of the battle. Louisa was shocked at her husband's idea. She questioned the wisdom of such an action, when everyone knew perfectly well that Jackson was also running for president and would therefore be her husband's chief political opponent.

Socially, intellectually, and physically, Andrew Jackson was the complete opposite of John Quincy. Jackson had little formal education. He had risen from poverty to become the owner of large plantations in Tennessee and a great military strategist. He was tall and lean, with a full and impressive head of wavy white hair. His thin face was lined with a vertical scar that he had received as a boy from a British soldier when he defied an order to shine the soldier's boots. The facial scar was not the only wound Jackson had suffered. Two bullets, one from a military action and another from a duel, were lodged in his body, causing him periodically to spit up bloody phlegm. This tough, self-made man was appealing to many Americans. His grit and determination seemed to speak to the average citizen, and his humble background reinforced his popularity. John Quincy represented the old aristocracy of New England, whose elitism only set him farther apart from the common man.

To deal with the issue of Jackson's widespread popularity, John Quincy formulated a scheme, which he confided to his wife. He wanted to convince the Tennessee war hero to be his running mate instead of his opponent. Having Jackson on his ticket as his vice-president would increase John Quincy's chances of winning the presidential race. John Quincy understood the importance and strength of the popular vote. As a young man, he had witnessed how the common people of France had elevated Napoléon from a general to an emperor. Besides, Jackson owed John Quincy a favor. Adams had been the only Cabinet member to support the general after his invasion of Florida. Louisa felt this was a good point, and she supported her husband's plan.

No expense was spared as the Adamses prepared to host the ball honoring Jackson. First they enlarged the dance floor of their Washington home. Then the rooms were hung with wreaths and lanterns, and the ballroom floor was decorated with chalk drawings of eagles, flags, military emblems, and an inscription saying "Welcome to the Hero of New Orleans".[2]

One thousand guests attended the affair. Some stood on chairs to catch a glimpse of General Jackson as he arrived on Louisa Adams's arm. The highlight of the evening occurred when one of the tiny hanging lamps tipped over, dripping oil down Louisa's neck and shoulder. Someone in the audience compared the incident to stories in the Bible where men who were to become king first had their heads anointed with sacred oil. The crowd

*On January 8, 1824, a ball was given by the Adamses in honor of General Andrew Jackson. About one thousand guests attended. From left to right, the men pictured here are John C. Calhoun, Daniel Webster, Andrew Jackson, Henry Clay, and John Quincy Adams.*

cheered, buzzing that the "anointment" was a good omen for an Adams presidential victory. Louisa reassured her guests that the oil was not sacred and that only her silver gown was spoiled. All the guests departed in good humor at around one-thirty in the morning.[3]

Although the Adams's ball was a success with their guests, John Quincy's scheme to woo Jackson to his ticket failed. Jackson decided to keep pursuing the presidency. President James Monroe had two other Cabinet members who were also interested in the post. Secretary of the Treasury William H. Crawford, a Virginian who was crippled by a stroke during his campaign, was also running. Secretary of War John C. Calhoun from South Carolina started out as a presidential contender but later accepted the nomination as the sole vice-presidential candidate. (At this time, a vice-president could be voted into office on his own, and a presidential candidate did not necessarily have to choose a running mate.) Besides these Cabinet members, Speaker of the House Henry Clay from Kentucky also sought the presidency.

All of the four final candidates ran on the strength of their personal accomplishments and claimed to be Democratic-Republicans, a party that believed in the sovereignty of the states. At this time there was only one party. John Quincy's Federalist party had faded away during the Monroe years.

In 1824 general elections were not held directly for president and vice-president in America. Instead voters chose electors, or special representatives, to vote for the presidential candidate of their choice at an assembly called the electoral college. Every state also held a popular vote in which white males were allowed to vote for president. Some states used these results to determine which candidate's electors would be chosen. Others allowed the state legislatures to choose the electors. Under the Constitution of the United States, these chosen electors would then choose the president in the electoral college. A presidential candidate needed 131 electoral votes to win.

In November 1824 eligible voters went to the election polls. When the presidential votes were finally tallied in December, Jackson had won the most popular votes with 153,544 votes. However, the electoral vote gave Jackson only 99 votes to Adams's 84, Crawford's 41, and Clay's 37.[4] No single presidential candidate had received the required majority of 131 electoral votes. The Twelfth Amendment to the Constitution stated that if no candidate had a clear majority, then the House of Representatives would choose the president from among the three top-scoring candidates. Therefore, Henry Clay was eliminated from the race. For close to two months, Adams, Jackson, and Crawford campaigned, but this time to House members only.

Henry Clay did not waste any time throwing his support to his old friend, John Quincy. Both men believed in a strong, united federal government and federally funded national programs. Clay gave parties and banquets in honor of his former partner at Ghent. The Jackson followers fumed and called Clay's obvious support of Adams "corrupt bargaining." They suspected that in return for his support, Clay had been promised a high position in the new administration if John Quincy were to win.

On January 9 and January 25, 1825, John Quincy and Clay met privately to discuss politics. They saw a country that was beginning to divide and weaken because of regional economic self-interests. The North's economy had become industrial, whereas the South's economy was primarily agricultural. To preserve the Union, John Quincy and Clay believed that the United States needed a strong central national government. Internal improvements, such as the construction of highways and canals, depended upon having such a strong central government. John Quincy and Clay's national stance contrasted sharply with that of the Democratic-Republican party, which believed in the sovereignty of the individual states, or strong state-ruled governments. This split in political ideology caused John Quincy's followers to call themselves National-Republicans. Jackson and Crawford remained Democratic-Republicans. Now, House members had two parties, and they could choose the candidate who expressed similar political interests.

A heavy snowfall blanketed the capital when the House of Representatives finally met to elect a president

*Cartoonist David Claypoole Johnson portrayed the three final candidates in the election of 1824—Adams, Jackson, and Treasury Secretary William Crawford—in a foot race to the White House.*

on the preset date, Wednesday, February 9, 1825. Each state received one vote, and the winner of that vote was determined by a majority of the congressmen from that state. Henry Clay had persuaded the majority of the representatives from Ohio and Kentucky to vote for Adams. However, New York's representatives were tied seventeen to seventeen.[5] When New York congressman Stephen Van Rensselaer trudged through the snow to cast his vote, Henry Clay was waiting for him. Clay invited Van Rensselaer into his office. He proceeded to explain the importance of his state's vote and how an Adams win was essential for the good of the country. Though he had initially supported Crawford, Van Rensselaer left Clay's office in tears, confused and visibly shaken.[6] America's future, it seemed, rested in the New Yorker's hands.

In times of great emergency, the old New York

congressman often bowed his head in prayer and asked God for guidance. He did so at this time. When Van Rensselaer opened his eyes, he saw on the floor a ticket bearing Adams's name. Regarding this ticket as a message from God, Van Rensselaer picked it up and placed it in the ballot box. Van Rensselaer's vote was significant. The New York tie was broken, giving John Quincy the majority vote of thirteen states to Jackson's seven and Crawford's four.[7] John Quincy Adams had become the sixth president of the United States. In his diary he wrote: "May the blessing of God rest upon the event of this day!"[8]

In Massachusetts, John Adams wept with joy.[9] It was the only time in American history that a father and son had both attained the high office of president of the United States. The ninety-year-old ex-president quickly wrote a letter to his friend Thomas Jefferson boasting about the news. Jefferson replied, "Every line from you exhilarates my spirit and gives a glow of pleasure. . . ."[10]

Tired but elated, John Quincy Adams took the oath of office in the hall of the House of Representatives on Friday March 4, 1825, along with the new vice-president, John C. Calhoun. John Quincy began his term by reappointing Monroe's talented Cabinet. Henry Clay had advised the president against this action. Clay suggested removing Monroe's Democratic-Republican Cabinet members, and instead selecting people who would support National-Republican policies. However, John Quincy believed that a person's ability rather than his party loyalty should qualify him for a job. He disregarded Clay's advice. John Quincy then appointed Henry Clay to be secretary of state. Jackson supporters were outraged! Quickly they spread rumors reminding people how Jackson had suspected "corrupt bargaining" all along between John Quincy and Clay. John Quincy paid no attention to these rumors. He knew firsthand that Clay's experience as an outstanding national and international negotiator qualified him for the Cabinet position. The new president denied all charges of corruption, but the damage was done. Andrew Jackson's revenge was just beginning.

A muddy road led to the president's Executive Mansion. Sheep, horses, and cows grazing on the grassy country grounds surrounded the home. Plumbing and running water did not exist in 1825. During President Monroe's administration, the exterior of the Executive Mansion had been painted white to cover up the burned discoloration caused when the British had set fire to it during the War of 1812. The Adamses soon discovered that although the exterior of the house now appeared new, the interior was still in shambles. The place was dirty and the furniture badly damaged. Louisa was so disgusted that she invited the public in to view the rundown condition of the Executive Mansion, or the White House as it was now nicknamed. Louisa's shrewd effort to persuade the public to call for the remodeling of the presidential home worked. Congress allotted a small amount of money to update and redecorate it.

It took six weeks before the Adamses could move from their F Street home to the newly renovated White House. Nineteen servants cared for the first family. Two nieces, Mary Hellen and Lizzie Adams, were summoned to help Louisa with party arrangements. John II, who had been expelled from Harvard for participating in a riot, served as his father's private secretary. The other two Adams sons remained in Massachusetts. George was a lawyer in

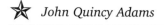 

Senator Daniel Webster's firm, and young Charles Francis was still attending Harvard.

On November 25, 1825, John Quincy read aloud to his Cabinet his first annual message to Congress. The message emphasized the proposal of federally funded programs to enrich the United States. It recommended internal improvements of and by the national government. These included the creation of a Department of the Interior, a reform of existing patent laws, the establishment of a uniform system of weights and measures, and the development and expansion of railroads and canals. To broaden man's knowledge, he suggested the establishment of a national university and a military academy, the financing of scientific exploration, and the building of astronomical observatories.

John Quincy's Cabinet members were alarmed! They cautioned the new president that such radical policies would undoubtedly anger Congress and the public. They even questioned whether his proposed policies were constitutional, and they refused to support his national programs. Clay's warning not to choose unsympathetic Cabinet members now seemed wise.

However, John Quincy ignored his Cabinet's advice. He strongly believed that his proposed policies were in the best interest of the nation. Certainly his countrymen would recognize their importance. On December 26, 1825, John Quincy presented his annual message to Congress despite its poor reception with the Cabinet.

A handwritten copy of the president's message was distributed to each member. Congress was horrified! It was the first time a president publicly supported national improvements. Members of Congress accused John

Quincy of being a monarchist, or someone who ruled his country like a king or queen. The newly formed country still feared a return of a monarchy like the British one they had just overthrown.

In addition, Congress and the public mocked John Quincy's ideas in the newspapers. They called his astronomical observatory "a light-house of the skies."[11] All these criticisms left the sixth president hurt and angry. For Jackson supporters, however, John Quincy's nationalistic message was a godsend; it provided exactly the kind of ammunition they needed to keep John Quincy from a second presidential term.

John Quincy was listening to patriotic speeches at the Capitol on July 4, 1826, the fiftieth anniversary of the signing of the Declaration of Independence. As the president listened, his ninety-one-year-old father, at home in Quincy, Massachusetts, was dying from old age. Although his body was giving out, John Adams remained mentally alert. To acknowledge the national holiday he told family members, "Independence forever!"[12] At around 1:00 P.M., John Adams told one of his granddaughters, "Jefferson still survives." Those were the last words he spoke. At 6:00 P.M., family members heard a clap of thunder just as they watched John Adams take his last breath.

What John Adams did not know was that his longtime friend, Thomas Jefferson, had also died that same day from a urinary disease at his Monticello home in Virginia. Ironically, the eighty-three-year-old Virginian died at 1:00 P.M., the exact time John Adams spoke his last words about his friend. Fittingly, the country lost two of its foremost citizens fifty years to the day after the signing of the Declaration of Independence. Both men had been

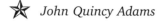 

patriots, authors of the Declaration of Independence, and presidents. Three days after the Fourth of July, John Quincy received messages containing word of the two deaths. That evening he wrote in his journal, "The time, the manner, the coincidence . . . are . . . marks of Divine favor."[13]

As early as October 1825, Andrew Jackson began running for the next presidential election, which wouldn't take place until three years later. Jackson's supporters created a new style of campaigning using catchy songs, slogans, and campaign buttons. When Jackson was a general, his soldiers, who admired his courage, had nicknamed him "Old Hickory," after the hickory tree, which is resilient and tough. To advertise this nickname, Jackson's followers passed out hickory sticks and canes across the country to arouse public interest in their candidate. Many newspapers continued to publish cartoons and articles mocking John Quincy's proposed nationalistic programs, and at the same time promoted Jackson's successful accomplishments as a general.

While Jackson's campaigners were working the public, his supporters in Congress were causing friction with the president. In the congressional election of 1826 Jackson's Democratic-Republicans became the majority party. For the first time in American history, the majority party was opposed to the president's administration. The lack of congressional support severely hampered John Quincy's ability to pass legislation on internal improvements. Repeatedly, the Democratic-Republicans turned down the president's plans for national improvements. Most members of Congress disapproved of President Adams and Secretary of State Clay's strong federal programs. Instead they favored state sovereignty, or the ability and rights of the individual states to govern their own programs. The completion of the Erie Canal by the state of New York on November 4, 1825, was used as an example of state-governed programs.

Congress never ceased trying to humiliate John Quincy. Its leaders wanted to make sure that, like his father, he would be a one-term president. That way they could bring back a form of government that favored states' rights. One of their tactics was to propose an unreasonable tariff, or tax.

By 1828 northern states had largely replaced farming with manufacturing. Northerners supported high tariffs on imported goods. If these foreign goods that were imported were taxed, they would become more expensive than the same goods produced locally. If they were more expensive, the imported goods would be less attractive to buyers. If more people bought domestic goods, the factories and businesses producing them would stay in business. On the other hand, farmers in southern states wanted very low tariffs on imported goods. The South was still primarily agricultural and sold cotton, one of its most important crops, to Great Britain. In return, manufactured goods from Great Britain were sold cheaply to the South. If these British goods were now heavily taxed, they would become more expensive. Southerners saw the tariff as opposing their self-interest.

Trying to trap John Quincy, Jackson's supporters in Congress wrote a bill raising taxes on any commodity any senator wanted protected. If the president signed the bill, it would anger the South. If he vetoed the bill or voted against it, he would alienate the North. John Quincy was placed in a no-win situation. Reluctantly, the president signed the bill in favor of the tariff, but he tried to blame its faults on Congress. However, both northerners and southerners blamed the president, and the "tariff of abominations," as it became known, definitively ruined John Quincy's chances for being reelected.

John Quincy's political setbacks were not his only problems. Family tragedies and disappointments also plagued him. George, his oldest son, had run up huge drinking and gambling debts. In addition, George's 1827 engagement to his cousin Mary Hellen was broken. While living in the White House, Mary had become attracted to George's brother, John II. This lovers' triangle had added intense tension to the Adams household. Both John Quincy and Louisa highly disapproved of Mary's change of heart. However, in the end, John II and Mary were married in the White House on February 28, 1828. Heartbroken, George did not attend the wedding.

With political and personal crises overrunning his life, John Quincy's spirits once again sank into a deep depression. He grew weak and moody. He lost his appetite, and his clothes hung loosely.[14] He also suffered from his old ailments of insomnia, indigestion, and palsy. Louisa, too, was sickly. She suffered from migraine headaches, fainting spells, and psychosomatic depression, which led to other illnesses and physical disorders caused by her emotions. She spent most of her White House days sick in bed.

John Quincy tried to snap out of his depression by attending three different Sunday church services: Unitarian, Presbyterian, and Episcopal. He continued his daily practice of reading the Bible in several different languages. By comparing various types of religions and biblical translations, he sought God's power over the heart. He continued writing in his journal in the hope of providing spiritual awakening for his soul.

As he had done so many years ago in Russia, John Quincy made four-mile walks a regular part of his routine daily exercise. Two hours before dawn, he would walk from the White House to the Capitol and back. At other times he walked to Georgetown and back. He always clocked himself, trying to decrease his time. During the steamy summer months, he switched from walking to swimming. At the age of fifty-eight, the president was such an expert swimmer that he was able to swim the width of the Potomac River in one hour. At a place where the Tiber and Potomac rivers flowed together stood an old sycamore tree and a large rock. The health-conscious president found this point in the river to be an ideal spot for diving and skinny-dipping.

Once a newspaperwoman named Anne Royall, who had been trying unsuccessfully to get an interview with the president, followed him to the river. While the president was skinny-dipping, Royall sat on his clothes and called out to him in the river. Startled, John Quincy asked the woman what she wanted. She told him she wanted an interview. John Quincy promised Royall that if she would hide in the bushes while he got dressed he would grant her the interview. However, Royall, wanting to make sure, sat firmly on the president's clothes and demanded the interview right then and there. Chin deep in the river and naked, John Quincy had no choice but to grant the newspaperwoman her wish.[15]

Despite John Quincy's efforts to heal his inner soul

through prayer and exercise, the fact remained that his chances for reelection looked grim. Toward the end of the campaign, the president's supporters became desperate. In a smear campaign worthy of today's sleaziest politicians, they dug up dirt from Jackson's past. Published in local newspapers, these articles accused Jackson of murder, adultery, and gambling at cockfights. Jackson did indeed gamble at cockfights, and he had killed a man during a duel, but it was legal at the time. As for adultery, Jackson had unknowingly married his wife, Rachel, before her divorce was final. The mudslinging, however, failed to tarnish his image as an American hero, and Andrew Jackson handily won the 1828 presidential election. On March 4, 1829, Andrew Jackson and his rowdy followers stormed into Washington, D.C., ransacking and throwing furniture from the recently decorated White House.

John Quincy and Louisa temporarily rented a home outside the capital. A month after Jackson's inauguration, Louisa wrote to her son George, asking him to help them move. They now planned to return to Quincy. George agreed to help his parents, but while he was making the sea voyage to Washington, D.C., the troubled young man began drinking heavily. According to passengers on his ship, he had been suffering from mood swings and deep depression. That night, George committed suicide by throwing himself overboard.[16] A month later the twenty-eight-year-old's body was found along the shore of New York's Long Island Sound. Grief-stricken, John Quincy and Louisa delayed their move.

History had repeated itself, yet again. Both John Adams and John Quincy Adams had traveled from the heights of achievement to the depths of despair: Both father and son had become leaders of their country. Both had lost a son to the ravages of alcoholism.

At the age of sixty-two, John Quincy was sure his political life was over. Like his father, he expected to retire to Quincy. Little did he know that a new and important phase of his political career was about to begin.

*George Washington Adams, John Quincy's oldest son, suffering from depression and alcohol abuse, threw himself overboard, drowning at the age of twenty-eight.*

# 10

# A BOY AGAIN

The summer after George's death, John Quincy returned to Quincy to attend his youngest son's wedding. On September 3, 1829, Charles Francis married Abigail Brooks, the daughter of a wealthy Bostonian. Still despondent over George's death, Louisa stayed in Washington and refused to attend the wedding. Not until later that fall would Louisa join her husband at the Big House, the home John Quincy inherited upon the death of his father.

Life was tense at the Big House. Both John Quincy and Louisa remained in a deep depression over their son's suicide. To make matters worse, a woman named Eliza Dolph claimed that George had fathered her child.[1] Although it was true, the Adamses did not believe the woman's allegation and refused to pay child support. They also worried about their second son, John II, who remained in

Washington, D.C., with his wife, Mary. Before Louisa left the capital, she noticed that John II had begun drinking heavily, and she feared that John's fate might end up tragically, like George's.

John Quincy tried finding pleasure in reading and planting tree seedlings, but his sadness was overwhelming. In his journal, he prayed to God for forgiveness and mercy for his unshakable depression.[2] His prayer was answered in September 1830, when the Reverend Joseph Richardson and John B. Davis, the editor of the *Boston Patriot*, paid a call on the former president. Reverend Richardson had decided to retire from his seat in Congress and return to his Unitarian parish. The two men were there to persuade John Quincy to run for Richardson's seat. Fearing that the ex-president might consider a congressman's position beneath his status, the two men had prepared a persuasive speech. They assured John Quincy that a victory would be easy and that his presence in Congress would dignify the House of Representatives.

John Quincy had been

*The Adams's youngest son, Charles Francis, was named after John Quincy's brother who died from the effects of alcohol abuse. Ironically, Charles Francis was the only Adams son not to die from this cause.*

the obedient son of two famous parents, a skillful diplomat, a short-term senator, a brilliant secretary of state, and a beaten president and father. Politically, he had done almost everything. Personally, he had nothing to lose. John Quincy was tired of constantly being depressed. Becoming a congressman sparked an adventuresome and interesting opportunity. The challenge seemed irresistible. By nature a public servant, John Quincy felt assured that by becoming a congressman he would finally fulfill his responsibility to his country and God. Thus, with excitement, he agreed to seek the office. John Quincy told Richardson and Davis, "No person could be degraded by serving the people as a Representative in Congress. Nor, in my opinion, would an ex-President of the United States be degraded by serving as a selectman of his town, if elected thereto by the people."[3]

Both his wife and Charles Francis reacted strongly when John Quincy Adams broke the news to them. How could he possibly consider becoming a congressman now? Wasn't his obsessive attention to his work what had driven George toward suicide? Hadn't he learned his lesson about the evils that result from too much work? Would it not now be more seemly for husband and father to retire graciously with his family like all the other ex-presidents?

Neither Louisa nor Charles Francis could understand John Quincy's reason for wanting to go back into politics. The whole idea appalled them. However, John Quincy ignored his family's pleas and ran for office. On November 1, 1830, John Quincy Adams, sixty-three years old, was easily elected to the twenty-second Congress. For the first time in his long political career, he attained political office by winning the popular vote. To angry family members he quoted Cicero: "I will not desert in my old age the Republic

I served in my youth."[4] In his journal he confessed, "No election or appointment . . . gave me so much pleasure."[5]

On March 4, 1831, John Quincy Adams assumed his seat in the House of Representatives. He was and still is the only former president in American history to serve in the House. Young politicians commonly begin their political careers as congressmen. John Quincy's odd reversal prompted Henry Clay to tease his longtime friend, asking what it was like to be a boy again.[6]

The "boy" congressman began his new career as chairman of the Committee on Manufacturing, essentially writing tariff bills. In an ironic twist of fate, he was asked to modify the tariff of abominations, the very bill the Jacksonians had created to bring about John Quincy's downfall as president. Southerners commonly tried to nullify, or refuse to pay, the tariff imposed by Congress. They claimed it was an infringement on the states' rights that were granted in the Tenth Amendment to the Constitution. President Jackson disagreed. If states could choose which federal laws to obey, then what was the purpose of the Union? For once, John Quincy and Jackson agreed. The Union must be preserved!

Beginning in May 1832, John Quincy worked on the tariff bill. Often he was the first congressman to arrive in the morning and the last to leave at night. After months of hard work, John Quincy had designed a compromise bill that reduced but did not eliminate the tariff. This tariff provided northerners with protection over their goods, at the same time allowing southerners access to free trade. The compromise bill passed, resolving a national crisis that could have split the Union. The tariff of abominations was overturned, and John Quincy became a congressional hero for managing to appease both sides.

While Congress was in session, John Quincy and Louisa lived at their F-Street home in Washington, D.C. John II, his wife Mary, and their two daughters lived with them. John II managed a gristmill in town owned by his father. Gradually, the mill started to lose money, and as it did John II's drinking increased. In October of 1834, John II died of alcoholism at the age of thirty-one. Louisa, who was still despondent over George's death, continued to blame her husband for her two sons' tragic deaths. She claimed that the demands of John Quincy's political career had resulted in neglect of their children. Sadness, anger, and a chilling tension filled the Adams home.[7]

Tension was also brewing in the United States. The most controversial issue was slavery. By 1836 the northern movement to abolish, or do away with, slavery had grown and was taking on a religious fervor. Anti-slavery sentiments were being preached all over the North in church sermons, fiery political speeches, and literature now being

*John Quincy's second son, John II Adams, who was named after his grandfather, died in October 1834, a victim of alcohol abuse like his brother George. John II was thirty-one years old.*

mass-produced by the new steam-powered presses. Congress began receiving numerous petitions to abolish slavery. A petition is a document formulated, requested, and signed by people, which attempts to make a new policy or change an existing one. The number of slavery-related petitions was so great that no other business was getting done in Congress.

Meanwhile, the South, whose agricultural economy depended on the existing system of slavery, became militant in its insistence on justifying the use of slaves. To squash the antislavery movement, Henry Laurens Pinckney of South Carolina proposed three resolutions in Congress. The first two stated that Congress would have no constitutional power to interfere with slavery in Washington, D.C., or in any state. The third resolution suggested that all petitions regarding the subject of slavery be silenced in the House. Pinckney and his supporters hoped that by silencing or stopping the discussions on slavery they would prevent the abolition of slavery by Congress.

In response to this third resolution, Congressman Adams rose and shouted angrily to the House that the third resolution was a "direct violation of the Constitution of the United States" that clearly states every man has the right to petition on any subject.[8] His father and other patriots had fought hard for this right. However, Congress approved and passed the resolution. It was now called the "gag rule."

Beginning in 1836, John Quincy battled the gag rule on the ground that all petitions, even antislavery petitions, should be honored and heard in Congress, as was provided for in the Constitution. However, he believed that pursuing a moral antislavery position at this time would destroy the country that his father helped create. Besides, thus far the abolitionist movement was relatively small in number and considered militant. If John Quincy took their side, Massachusetts voters would probably vote him out of office.

John Quincy's indecisive stance angered both southern supporters of slavery and abolitionists. Southerners viewed his stance on allowing antislavery petitions in Congress as a threat to their lifestyle. However, the abolitionists considered Congressman Adams's position on allowing antislavery petitions too weak. They wanted him to fight not merely the gag rule, but the inhumanity of slavery itself. Nevertheless, despite his weak moral stance on slavery, the abolitionists decided to use John Quincy to advance their movement. They knew that the old congressman was feisty, outspoken, and unconcerned about his reputation. He was also an ex-president, who could arouse the public interest necessary to bring attention to the abolitionists' cause.

Privately, John Quincy was an opponent of slavery. He wanted the United States to live up to the principles

## SOURCE DOCUMENT

*John Quincy's motion to amend the House journal on the gag rule was made in writing on May 27, 1836.*

described in the Constitution stating that "all men are created equal." He wanted all men to enjoy the rights of "life, liberty, and the pursuit of happiness." In 1790, Massachusetts officially abolished slavery, and John Quincy proudly noted this fact in his journal. Along with this notation, John Quincy also wrote down his innermost feelings about the issue of slavery: "Oh, if but one man could arise," he wrote, "now is the time, and this is the occasion, upon which such a man would perform the duties of an angel upon earth."[9]

In January 1837, when Congress reconvened, John Quincy considered the gag rule to be merely a challenging obstacle. Using parliamentary rules, he found clever ways to present petitions before Congress. Under parliamentary rules, each congressman was allowed to state the contents of his state's citizens' petitions, beginning with Maine and moving southward. When it was John Quincy's turn, he presented three petitions from women in Massachusetts. The first petition, calling for the end of slavery, had been written and signed by 150 women from Dorchester. The former president pleaded with his fellow congressmen to listen to " . . . the greatest improvement that can possibly be effected in the condition of the human race—the total abolition of slavery on earth."[10] Quickly, the House voted down this first petition.

Undaunted, the seventy-year-old congressman pressed on and read a petition by women from South Weymouth which expressed the sinfulness of slavery. Congressman Henry Laurens Pinckney from South Carolina jumped to his feet and asked Speaker of the House James Polk if the gentleman from Massachusetts had a right, under the gag rule, to read the petition?[11]

The speaker of the House sided with the Massachusetts congressman but reminded him to keep his statements on each petition brief. John Quincy continued reading, "immediately to abolish slavery in the District of Columbia."[12]

"A call to order!" shouted a congressman.

The speaker of the House told John Quincy to sit down.

Still reading the petition while easing into his chair, Congressman Adams bellowed in his notorious high shrill voice, "and to declare every human being free who sets foot upon its soil."[13]

John Quincy continued to push the limits of testing the gag rule. He hurled personal insults at his opponents, as he attacked the morality of these southern congressmen. The old Massachusetts congressman had a plan. By purposely provoking the southern members of the House, he sought to anger the southerners enough to motivate them into asking for his removal from the House. John Quincy knew that once attacked, parliamentary rules allowed him to claim the floor in his own defense, thus giving him the chance to say anything he wanted to say. His plan worked, and a motion was called for, requesting his removal from the House. Then, instead of defending his behavior, John Quincy chose to present his antislavery petitions, about which the gag rule would otherwise have prevented him from speaking. After his presentation, he informed the speaker of the House that he would need a week to complete his defense, or the House could dismiss the motion to remove him. To avoid wasting the House's time on such a minor issue, the speaker of the House chose the latter course of action: Congress dismissed its motion to remove him, and John Quincy remained a congressman. This outcome only further enraged the congressmen who had demanded his removal.

John Quincy did not always have to trick the House into listening to the slavery debate. From time to time, other topics under discussion called for an assessment of the merits and demerits of slavery. Such was the case in 1838, when the House considered annexing the Republic of Texas, or making it part of the United States, since it had declared its independence from Mexico in 1836. John Quincy knew that slavery was an accepted practice in Texas. He feared that, if annexed, Texas would eventually become a slave state, thus tipping the balance to more slave states than free. At this time, the United States had twelve free states and twelve slave states.

Using the strategy of a filibuster, or a very lengthy speech meant to delay proceedings, Congressman Adams viciously attacked slavery from June 16 to July 7 through

*British artist Robert Cruikshank's engraving shows House members fighting over the gag rule. This fight was John Quincy's most impassioned issue during his years in Congress.*

a combination of petitions and his own hostile speeches. He still opposed the gag rule and defended the right to petition, but now he openly denounced slavery as a moral issue, as well. In one speech he said, "I do believe slavery to be a sin before the sight of God and that is the reason and the only . . . reason why we should not annex Texas to the Union."[14] Since the main issue was the annexation of Texas, and not the issue of slavery itself, he could get around the gag rule and officially discuss slavery. John Quincy's stalling tactic worked. The exasperated Congress adjourned for the summer without ever getting the chance to vote on the annexation of Texas.

Hate and threatening letters poured in daily. On one occasion, a colored lithograph of John Quincy was marked with a bullet hole on the forehead. Opponents dubbed him "the madman from Massachusetts." Louisa feared for her husband's safety, but John Quincy was relentless, never retreating in the face of controversy and thriving on attacking confrontational issues.[15]

John Quincy's arguments infuriated many, but he had many admirers, as well. Some rewarded him with an ivory cane. The yard-long white cane tipped in sterling silver was made from a single elephant's tusk. Its handle featured a gold-inlaid American eagle bearing a scroll with the motto "Right of Petition Triumphant." Inscribed beneath the handle were the words "John Quincy Adams" and "*Justum et Tenacem propositi virum,*" which is Latin for "The just and firm of purpose."[16] Though deeply touched, John Quincy firmly believed that government officials should never accept gifts. Thus he entrusted the cane to the care of the Patent Office.

In 1839, an international slave incident became a

controversial topic in the United States. The incident involved Africans from the Mendi tribe who were illegally captured and taken to Havana, Cuba. According to the Anglo-Spanish treaty of 1817, new slaves could not be imported into Spanish-owned Cuba after 1817. However, slaves already there were to remain slaves.

Two Cubans, Jose Ruiz and Pedro Montes, bought the Mendi Africans to be their slaves. They made them false passports and set out to transport them to Puerto Prinicipe, Cuba, under cover of darkness aboard the ship *Amistad*.[17] Frightened for his life, Cinqué, one of the Mendi Africans onboard the *Amistad*, unlocked his chains with a nail, and then freed the other captives. The Mendi Africans revolted and killed all but two of the ship's Spanish crewmen. Then Cinqué ordered the two surviving Spaniards to navigate the *Amistad* back to Africa. However, by changing the ship's course at night, the Spanish sailors tricked the Africans and sailed to Long Island, New York, where the United States Navy intercepted them. The navy seized the vessel, freed the two Spaniards, and eventually took the Mendi Africans to New Haven, Connecticut, where they were held in a jail to determine whether they should be considered slaves or freemen.

For two years the Mendi captives sat in jail awaiting their fate. Abolitionists and Yale divinity students visited the jail regularly and tried to teach them English and Christianity. An attorney named Roger S. Baldwin was assigned to defend them. Evidence he presented showed that the Mendi Africans were illegally captured under the terms of the 1817 treaty, and he won the case.

Despite this victory, the Mendi Africans were not freed. President Martin Van Buren, who was seeking reelection, feared the South's reaction to the decision in the case. Along with many newspaper editors, Van Buren wanted the Mendi Africans turned back, or extradited, to Cuba. His administration submitted an appeal to the Supreme Court, hoping to have the decision reversed.

Like many other Americans, John Quincy followed the trial through the newspapers. Then one day Lewis Tappan, one of the founders of the American Anti-Slavery Society, asked John Quincy, who was still an attorney, to assist defense lawyers already defending thirty-nine Africans before the United States Supreme Court. Tappan hoped that the publicity generated by an outspoken ex-president would increase public awareness and sympathy for the antislavery movement. Reluctantly, John Quincy accepted Tappan's request to help with the defense. His last appearance before a court had been thirty-three years ago. By now John Quincy had forgotten many courtroom procedures, and he lacked confidence in his legal skills. For weeks, he worried about how he would argue this case.[18]

On February 22, 1842, the *Amistad* case, as it was now called, was tried in the basement under the Senate chambers. John Quincy presented his defense of the Africans to the Supreme Court. For two days, he delivered an eloquent argument, stressing natural law and the fundamental human right of liberty. He also attacked the Van Buren administration's attempt to force unlawfully seized Africans into slavery. John Quincy had transformed the Supreme Court into a "theater of great interest and attracted a crowded audience."[19] Justice Joseph Story called John Quincy's arguments extraordinary.

Finally, the Supreme Court declared that the Mendi Africans were not slaves, and that they were to be set free.

*The room in the Senate chambers where John Quincy tried the* Amistad *case is preserved for public viewing.*

In gratitude, they presented John Quincy with a Bible before returning to Africa as missionaries. Later, Tappan and other abolitionists published and used John Quincy's arguments in the case as propaganda against slavery. Every member of Congress also received a copy of John Quincy's arguments. Although the *Amistad* victory took on great importance, Lewis Tappan never received a bill from his cocounsel, the ex-president.

As public awareness of the slavery issue spread, John Quincy's popularity soared, especially in the North and West. The *Amistad* case brought him fame, and people wanted to see and hear John Quincy speak.

During the summer of 1843, John Quincy traveled to Niagara Falls with his daughter-in-law, Abigail Brooks, and his grandson, John Quincy II. The trip was meant for relaxation, but all along the train's route, people gathered, listened, and cheered "Old Man Eloquent," as his admirers now fondly called him. Later that year John Quincy journeyed to Cincinnati, where a wide banner strung across Sixth Street read: "John Quincy Adams, the Defender of the Rights of Man."[20] There he proudly laid the cornerstone of the Cincinnati Observatory. Astronomy had always been a subject dear to his heart.

At the beginning of each congressional session, a congressman would propose that amendments from the previous congressional session be adopted for the upcoming session. House members would then motion for or against each proposed amendment before voting on it. Ever since 1836, when the gag rule amendment was brought to the House floor, Congressman Adams would strongly condemn the rule and make a motion to have it abolished. In 1844, to the seventy-seven-year-old congressman's surprise, the motion passed! That night he wrote in his journal: "Blessed, forever blessed, be the name of God."[21] For eight years, John Quincy had battled the House. Gradually, support for the gag rule dwindled. People who were not abolitionists also began to understand the dangers of the rule. Congressmen recognized this change and voted accordingly. At once, John Quincy retrieved the ivory cane from the Patent Office and had the repeal date of the gag rule, December 3, 1844, engraved on its handle. Then he formally presented the cane to the people of the United States.

The cane was not the only gift Americans would receive through the efforts of John Quincy. In 1829 an eccentric British chemist named James Smithson bequeathed to the United States a gift of more than five hundred thousand dollars in gold. His will contained instructions to use the money to construct a building that would be used to increase the knowledge of man. It would be called the Smithsonian Institution, after Mr. Smithson. No one knows why this Englishman decided to give the United States such a generous gift.

For several years the funds were held by members of Congress, because they questioned whether the federal government had the authority to accept the gift. In Congress, John Quincy convinced his fellow congressmen to consider accepting the gift, and in turn they chose him to chair the Smithsonian committee. Always interested in science, John Quincy gladly accepted the position. He felt that scientific knowledge could improve man's standard of living. As president, he had pressured Congress to provide national financing for the sciences, but he had failed. Now he would have a chance to help shape this goal. John Quincy had been a congressman for five years when he was chosen to chair the committee, and for ten more years he chaired it.

Finally, on April 28, 1846, he influenced Congress to pass a bill to distribute money for the construction of the Smithsonian Institution, which would house scientific equipment, a chemical laboratory, a library, an art gallery, and a lecture room. John Quincy had finally succeeded in establishing national funding for the sciences.

John Quincy was not always successful in Congress. His fight to keep Texas out of the Union ultimately failed. Texas proclaimed itself an independent republic that wanted to become part of the United States. On December 29, 1845, the United States obliged Texas's wish, and Texas became the twenty-eighth state under President

James Polk's administration. The United States' annexation of Texas angered Mexico, which still claimed Texas as its possession. The dispute over who owned Texas caused the United States to declare war on Mexico. A year later the Mexican War was won, and a peace treaty stating that Texas belonged to the United States was signed.

Texas was not John Quincy's only failing; his health was failing, too. In November 1847, John Quincy suffered a mild stroke while walking with his friend George Parkman. The stroke left the old man's body feeble, but his mind was fine. For several weeks he rested from his congressional work. He continued keeping his journal by dictating his words to Louisa. When he returned to the House on December 6, he received a standing ovation. Too weak to speak or write, the old congressman's work was limited, yet he relentlessly took his seat each congressional day.

On February 21, 1848, the House considered awarding medals to several generals in the Mexican War. When it came to call upon John Quincy Adams to vote for or against the medals, he bellowed out a firm "No!" Immediately, he flushed at the temples, clutched his desk, and slumped over. One congressman who saw what was happening shouted out a warning, while another managed to catch the old man before he toppled to the ground. The eighty-year-old congressman had suffered another stroke. Quickly, he was carried to the speaker's chambers. There, in a weak voice, he asked to see his old friend Henry Clay, who tearfully appeared, keeping his old friend company. A few minutes later John Quincy murmured, "This is the end of earth, but I am composed."[22] Then he slipped into a coma, and two days later he died, still lying inside the chamber of the speaker of the House.

*On February 21, 1848, Adams suffered a massive stroke at his seat in the House of Representatives. Too ill to be moved, he was carried to a sofa in the speaker's chambers where he lingered, then died two days later. Artist Arthur Stansbury drew this eyewitness sketch of the dying ex-president.*

After his death, John Quincy Adams's body was placed in a silver-mounted coffin surrounded by evergreen boughs and flowers. The coffin lay in state in front of the speaker of the House's platform, a raised seat inside the Capitol. On February 25 funeral services were held in Congress. Louisa was too bereaved to attend. Only a year before she and her husband had celebrated their fiftieth anniversary with family members.

A week later one member of Congress from each of the thirty states escorted the body on the five-hundred-mile train ride from the nation's capital to Quincy, Massachusetts. There John Quincy Adams's remains were placed in the family tomb across the road from Quincy's

First Parish Church. From the top of Penn's Hill, the place where Johnny and his mother had watched the Battle of Bunker Hill, guns fired a fitting salute.

In 1828, John Quincy had transferred John and Abigail Adams's remains into a granite sarcophagus inside the basement crypt of the First Parish Church. In December 1852, Charles Francis did the same for his parents. Louisa had died on May 15, 1852, at the age of seventy-seven. The only first lady born in a foreign land had become increasingly weak and frail after her husband's death.

In 1891 the First Parish Church, sometimes referred to as the church of presidents, began to allow visitors to see the crypt. It still contains the remains of two Adams presidents and first ladies. Today it remains a national shrine.

*The First Parish Church in Quincy, Massachusetts. John Quincy and Louisa Adams and his parents, John and Abigail, are all buried in a crypt in the church's basement.*

# 11

# LEGACY

John Quincy Adams's eulogy read, "Death found him at the post of duty; and where else could it have found him?"[1] For over sixty years, John Quincy was driven by a sense of duty to God, his country, and the honor of his father's name. John Adams and John Quincy Adams are the only father and son ever to both become president of the United States. John Quincy was the only former president to become a congressman. No other American served in more of the nation's highest positions.

John Quincy Adams was a world traveler and an intellectual. As a child, John Quincy began a journal and continued writing in it until his death. This famous journal still continues to fascinate historians; it is filled with detailed information on a period of American and European history spanning seventy years. It gives modern readers an eyewitness account of historical and social events across two continents. John Quincy spoke nine languages and in them he read the Bible, the classics, and contemporary literature. He loved to discuss political theories and current events, and he always remained up-to-date on international law. John Quincy was also intrigued by high-level mathematics, and his congressional report on weights and measurements remains, according to historian Paul C. Nagel, the finest evaluation on the subject ever produced.[2] John Quincy believed that knowledge is power, and he applied this power to the problems of a young nation.

Historian Greg Russell regarded John Quincy Adams as America's greatest foreign diplomat and secretary of state. According to Russell, John Quincy's universal intellect, Christian faith, and moral virtue molded him to earn this honor.[3] As a boy, while assisting his father in Europe, John Quincy received an unusual education in European politics and diplomacy. Years later, he was able to apply this unique knowledge. When America began to assert itself internationally, John Quincy expertly managed foreign affairs and helped define the role and shape the power of the newly formed United States.

During the "Golden Age of American Diplomacy" (1814–1825), John Quincy negotiated the Transcontinental Treaty with Spain. This treaty annexed East Florida and, for the first time, expanded the territory of the United States to the Pacific Ocean. Historian Samuel F. Bemis commented that the Transcontinental Treaty was "the greatest diplomatic victory won by any individual in the history of the United States."[4] John Quincy considered this diplomatic deal one of his finest accomplishments.

In 1823 he helped formulate the Monroe Doctrine,

ending two centuries of European colonization of the Western Hemisphere. This doctrine brilliantly established the United States as a nation of equal standing among other nations. It established the security of Western Hemisphere nations within their own boundaries and asserted their right of national independence. The Monroe Doctrine continues to be an important standard in American foreign policy. As recently as 1962, President John F. Kennedy invoked the doctrine to demand the removal of Russian nuclear weapons from Cuba.

Although John Quincy Adams was a successful diplomat and statesman, his presidency was filled with opposition and problems. He was the first president to urge the federal government to finance internal improvements. This national plan was an effort to better mankind and to unite a country that was beginning to fracture from sectional self-interest. Few Americans understood his reasoning. At the time of his presidency, America had only been in existence for fifty years. Most Americans feared a strong central government like the oppressive one they had just experienced under British colonial rule. Instead, many strongly defended states' rights, and Congress repeatedly vetoed the president's proposals.

John Quincy described his presidency by saying, "The great object of my life . . . failed."[5] Historian Paul C. Nagel agrees. Nagel has commented that John Quincy's "administration was a hapless failure and best forgotten."[6] Historian Walter A. McDougall, too, rates John Quincy's presidency as below average. McDougall agrees with other historians that John Quincy was "the greatest secretary of state in American history, but he was a bust as a president. He accomplished little, and left office embittered."[7]

Despite his presidential failures, however, this patriot's sense of duty to his country never wavered. As a congressman, John Quincy guided the creation and building of the Smithsonian Institution, a national science museum, and his personal dream. Other national improvements came only after his death. Today railroads, canals, and turnpikes span the continent. Scientific exploration continues to reach deep into the oceans and to far distant galaxies. Although they are not metric, our standards of weights and measures are uniform. These are all examples of John Quincy Adams's "failed" presidency. From the beginning of America's history, the hardworking New Englander obediently and repeatedly strove to improve his country.

*This statue of Abigail and seven-year-old John Quincy Adams witnessing the Battle of Bunker Hill is found in front of the First Parish Church in Quincy, Massachusetts.*

# Timeline

1767—Born July 11, the second child of John and Abigail Adams, in Braintree (now Quincy), Massachusetts.

1775—Witnessed the battle of Bunker Hill on June 17.

1778—Accompanied his father to France at age eleven.
–1779

1780—Accompanied his father to the Netherlands at age thirteen.

1781—Appointed secretary and French interpreter to Francis Dana, ambassador to Russia, at age fourteen.

1783—Returned to France. Appointed secretary to John Adams, who headed the negotiations on the Treaty of Paris.

1785—Began his diary on January 12.

1786—Admitted to Harvard College as a junior.

1787—Graduated from Harvard, second in his class, on July 16.

1790—Admitted to practice law in Massachusetts. Opened law office in Boston.

1791—Wrote *Publicola* letters and Marcellus and Columbus
–1793  articles.

1794—Served as minister to the Netherlands.

1797—Married Louisa Catherine Johnson in London on July 26.

1797—Served as ambassador to Prussia; signed Prussian-
–1802  American Maritime Treaty.

1801—Birth of first son, George Washington, on April 12.

1802—Elected to the Massachusetts state senate.

1803—Birth of John Adams II on July 4.

1803—Elected to United States Senate by the Massachu-
–1807  setts legislature.

1807—Birth of third son, Charles Francis, on August 18.

1809—Served as minister to Russia.
–1814

1811—Birth of daughter, Louisa Catherine, who died in infancy.

1814—Appointed to peace commission with Great Britain; signed Treaty of Ghent ending the War of 1812.

1815—Served as ambassador to Great Britain.
–1817

1817—Appointed secretary of state by President James Monroe.

1819—Signed the Transcontinental Treaty with Spain, annexing Florida.

1823—Under President Monroe helped formulate and write the Monroe Doctrine.

1825—Elected and served one term as president.
–1829

1829—Oldest son, George, died from drowning on April 30.

1829—Retired to Quincy, Massachusetts.

1830—Nominated to the House of Representatives.

1831—Served in the House of Representatives.
–1848

1834—Second son, John II, died from the complications of alcoholism on October 23.

1835—Chaired the Smithsonian Institution for ten years.
–1845

1836—Gag rule placed in effect over Adams's objection.

1841—Appealed *Amistad* case before United States Supreme Court and won.

1844—Gag rule abolished.

1846—Congress passed Smithsonian Institution bill.

1848—Died at the age of eighty in the House of Representatives on February 23.

1852—Louisa Adams died on May 15.

1852—Charles Francis Adams transferred the remains of John Quincy and Louisa Adams to a granite crypt beneath the First Parish Church, "the Church of Presidents," in Quincy, Massachusetts, on December 15.

# Chapter Notes

## Chapter 1. Bunker Hill

1. Jack Shepherd, *The Adams Chronicles* (Boston: Little Brown and Company, 1975), p. 68.

2. Paul C. Nagel, *John Quincy Adams* (New York: Alfred A. Knopf, 1997), p. 7.

## Chapter 2. To Be a Patriot

1. Phyllis Lee Levin, *Abigail Adams* (New York: St. Martins Press, 1987), p. 7.

2. Paul C. Nagel, *John Quincy Adams* (New York: Alfred A. Knopf, 1997), p. 7.

3. Marie B. Hecht, *John Quincy Adams* (Newtown, Conn.: American Political Biography Press, 1972), p. 10.

4. Ibid., p. 18.

5. Charles Aker, *Abigail Adams: An American Woman* (Boston: Little Brown and Company, 1980), p. 58.

6. Natalie Bober, *Abigail Adams: Witness to a Revolution* (New York: Atheneum Books for Young Readers, 1995), p. 59.

## Chapter 3. Lessons Abroad

1. Natalie Bober, *Abigail Adams: Witness to a Revolution* (New York: Atheneum Books for Young Readers, 1995), p. 91.

2. Page Smith, *John Adams* (New York: Doubleday and Company, Inc., 1962), p. 359.

3. Ibid., p. 433.

4. Ibid., p. 469.

5. Paul C. Nagel, *John Quincy Adams* (New York: Alfred A. Knopf, 1997), p. 23.

6. Worthington Ford, *Writings of John Quincy Adams* (New York: The Macmillan Company, 1913), p. 11.

7. Ibid., p. 8.

## Chapter 4. Changes

1. Marie B. Hecht, *John Quincy Adams* (Newtown, Conn.: American Political Biography Press, 1972), p. 50.

2. Paul C. Nagel, *John Quincy Adams* (New York: Alfred A. Knopf, 1997), p. 65.

3. Hecht, p. 74.

4. Jack Shepherd, *The Adams Chronicles* (Boston: Little, Brown and Company, 1975), p. 173.

## Chapter 5. A Diplomat

1. Paul C. Nagel, *John Quincy Adams* (New York: Alfred A. Knopf, 1997), p. 81.

2. Adams National Historic Site, biography on John Quincy Adams, p. 3.

3. Adams National Historic Site, chronology on John Quincy Adams, p. 2.

4. Marie B. Hecht, *John Quincy Adams* (Newtown: Conn., American Political Biography Press, 1972), p. 103.

5. Ibid., p. 117.

## Chapter 6. Senator Adams

1. Jack Shepherd, *The Adams Chronicles* (Boston: Little, Brown and Company, 1975), p. 220.

2. Marie B. Hecht, *John Quincy Adams* (Newtown, Conn.: American Political Biography Press, 1972), p. 141.

3. Ibid.

4. Adams National Historic Site, biography on John Quincy Adams, p. 3.

## Chapter 7. A Diplomat's Exile

1. Paul C. Nagel, *John Quincy Adams* (New York: Alfred A. Knopf, 1997), p. 185.

2. Paul C. Nagel, *The Adams Women* (New York: Oxford University Press, 1987), p. 184.

3. Ibid., p. 183.

4. Jack Shepherd, *The Adams Chronicles* (Boston: Little Brown and Company, 1975), p. 237.

5. Ibid., p. 238.

6. Robert Remini, *Henry Clay: Statesman of the Union* (New York: W. W. Norton & Company, 1991), p. 113.

7. Worthington Ford, *Writings of John Quincy Adams* (Boston: The Macmillan Company, 1913), p. 66.

8. Remini, p. 117.

9. Shepherd, p. 244.

## Chapter 8. Secretary of State

1. Marie B. Hecht, *John Quincy Adams* (Newtown, Conn.: American Political Biography Press, 1972), p. 289.

2. Allan Nevins, *The Diary of John Quincy Adams* (New York: Charles Scribner's Sons, 1951), pp. 211–213.

3. Paul C. Nagel, *John Quincy Adams* (New York: Alfred A. Knopf, 1997), p. 329.

4. Ibid., p. 263.

5. Ibid.

6. Jack Shepherd, *The Adams Chronicles* (Boston: Little, Brown and Company, 1975), p. 277.

7. Hecht, pp. 366–367.

## Chapter 9. Like Father, Like Son

1. Jack Shepherd, *The Adams Chronicles* (Boston: Little, Brown and Company, 1975), p. 267.

2. Allan Nevins, *The Diary of John Quincy Adams* (New York: Charles Scribner's Sons, 1951), p. 314.

3. Shepherd, p. 280.

4. Ibid., p. 281.

5. Robert Remini, *Henry Clay: Statesman of the Union* (New York: W. W. Norton & Company, 1991), p. 263.

6. Nevins, pp. 341–342.

7. Ibid., p. 341.

8. Page Smith, *John Adams* (New York: Doubleday and Company, Inc., 1962), p. 1135.

9. Ibid.

10. Shepherd, p. 285.

11. Ibid., p. 295.

12. Ibid.

13. Nevins, p. 360.

14. Marie B. Hecht, *John Quincy Adams* (Newtown, Conn.: American Political Biography Press, 1972), p. 453.

15. Shepherd, p. 302.

16. Paul C. Nagel, *John Quincy Adams* (New York: Alfred A. Knopf, 1997), p. 329.

## Chapter 10. A Boy Again

1. Marie B. Hecht, *John Quincy Adams* (Newtown, Conn.: American Political Biography Press, 1972), p. 453.

2. Paul Nagel, *John Quincy Adams* (New York: Alfred A. Knopf, 1997), p. 330.

3. Allan Nevins, *The Diary of John Quincy Adams* (New York: Charles Scribner's Sons, 1951), p. 405.

4. Jack Shepherd, *The Adams Chronicles* (Boston: Little, Brown and Company, 1975), p. 317.

5. Nevins, p. 406.

6. Robert Remini, *Henry Clay: Statesman of the Union* (New York: W. W. Norton & Company, 1991), p. 387.

7. Shepherd, p. 322.

8. Ibid., p. 326.

9. William Lee Miller, *Arguing About Slavery* (New York: Alfred A. Knopf, 1996), p. 185.

10. Shepherd, p. 327.

11. Ibid.

12. Ibid., p. 328.

13. Ibid.

14. Marie B. Hecht, *John Quincy Adams* (Newtown, Conn.: American Political Biography Press, 1972), p. 562.

15. Ibid., pp. 593–594.

16. Nevins, pp. 574–575.

17. "Timeline: Amistad Revolt," Mystic Seaport, Inc., 1997, <http://amistad.mysticseaport.org/timeline/amistad.html> (November 29, 1999).

18. Leonard Richards, *The Life and Times of Congressman Adams* (New York: Oxford University Press, 1986), p. 137.

19. Ibid.

20. Shepherd, p. 338.

21. Nevins, p. 573.

22. Hecht, p. 341.

## Chapter 11. Legacy

1. William Lee Miller, *Arguing About Slavery* (New York: Alfred A. Knopf, 1996), p. 167.

2. Paul C. Nagel, *John Quincy Adams* (New York: Alfred A. Knopf, 1997), p. 265.

3. Greg Russell, *John Quincy Adams and the Public Virtues of Diplomacy* (Columbia: University of Missouri Press, 1995), p. 3.

4. Marie B. Hecht, *John Quincy Adams* (Newtown, Conn.: American Political Biography Press, 1972), p. 300.

5. Jack Shepherd, *The Adams Chronicles* (Boston: Little, Brown and Company, 1975), p. 285.

6. Nagel, p. 296.

7. Walter A. McDougall, *New York National Review: Rating the Presidents*, vol. 49, no. 20, October 27, 1997, p. 33.

# Further Reading

Aker, Charles. *Abigail Adams: An American Woman*. Boston: Little, Brown and Company, 1980.

Bobbe, Dorothie. *Mr. and Mrs. John Quincy Adams: An Adventure in Patriotism*. New York: Minton, Balch & Co., 1930.

Bober, Natalie. *Abigail Adams: Witness to a Revolution*. New York: Atheneum Books for Young Readers, 1995.

Butterfield, L. H. *The Book of Abigail and John: Selected Letters of the Adams Family*. Cambridge, Mass.: Harvard University Press, 1975.

Ford, Worthington. *Writings of John Quincy Adams*. New York: The Macmillan Company, 1913.

Harness, Cheryl. *Young John Quincy*. New York: Simon and Schuster, 1994.

Hecht, Marie B. *John Quincy Adams*. Newtown, Conn.: American Political Biography Press, 1972.

Joseph, Paul. *John Quincy Adams*. Minneapolis, Minn.: ABDO Publishing Company, 1999.

Levin, Phyllis Lee. *Abigail Adams*. New York: St. Martin's Press, 1987.

Nagel, Paul C. *John Quincy Adams*. New York: Alfred A. Knopf, 1997.

Nagel, Paul C. *The Adams Women*. New York: Oxford University Press, 1987.

Nevins, Allan. *The Diary of John Quincy Adams 1794–1845*. New York: Charles Scribner's Sons, 1951.

Old, Wendie. *James Monroe*. Springfield, N.J.: Enslow Publishers, Inc., 1998.

Osborne, Angela. *Abigail Adams*. New York: Chelsea House Publishers, 1989.

Richards, Greg. *John Quincy Adams and the Public Virtues of Diplomacy*. Columbia: University of Missouri Press, 1995.

# Places to Visit and Internet Addresses

## Quincy, Massachusetts

*Adams National Historic Site*. Phone: (617) 770-1175. Located in the Presidents Place Galleria. Guided bus tours taking visitors to John Adams and John Quincy Adams birthplaces and to the Old House start here. Open seven days a week, April 19–November 10.

*First Parish Church and Adams Crypt*. Phone: (617) 773-1290. This is also referred to as the "the Church of Presidents" because both John Adams and John Quincy Adams are buried here with their wives. It is a national shrine. Open April 19–November 10.

*Adams Academy Building*. Phone: (617) 773-1144. This is the location of the Quincy Historical Society. It houses a museum and a research library where one can find out more about the Adams family and the town history.

## C-Span
<http://www.american presidents.org/presidents/
    presidents.asp?PresidentNumber=6>

## National Archives and Records Administration
<http://www.nara.gov.guide/index.html>
<http://www.nara.gov/education/teaching/amistad/jqa.html>

## Presidential Facts
<http://www/usahistory.com/presidents/jo–q–ad.htm>

## Waypages.com™
<http://www.waypages.com/history/US/presidents/John_
    Quincy_Adams.htm>

## The White House—John Quincy Adams
<http://www.whitehouse.gov/WH/glimpse/presidents/html/
    ja6.html>

# Index